19.91

MW01222712

Gateways:
Airports of Canada

Peter Pigott

Pottersfield Press
Lawrencetown Beach, Nova Scotia, Canada

Copyright © Peter Pigott 1996

All rights reserved. No part of this publication may be reproduced or transmitted in any form or by any means, electronic or mechanical, including photocopying, or by any information storage or retrieval system, without permission in writing from the publisher.

Canadian Cataloguing in Publication Data

Pigott, Peter
    Gateways
    ISBN 0-919001-96-3
1. Airports — Canada.   2. Aeronautics — Canada.   I. Title
HE9797.5.C3P53 1996   387.7'36'0971   C95-950340-4

Cover Photograph: Vancouver International Airport. (Photo courtesy Transport Canada)

Pottersfield Press gratefully acknowledges the ongoing support of the Nova Scotia Department of Education, Cultural Affairs Division, as well as the Canada Council and the Department of Canadian Heritage.

Printed and bound in Canada

Pottersfield Press
Lawrencetown Beach
R.R. 2 Porters Lake
Nova Scotia, Canada, B0J 2S0

Contents

Acknowledgements   5

Introduction   7

Early Days   10

History of Airports in Canada   15

Calgary   53

Edmonton   56

Gander   64

Goose Bay   72

Halifax   76

Hamilton   80

Montreal   86

Airports of the Northwest   103

Ottawa   108

Quebec City   117

Regina   120

Toronto   122

Vancouver   138

Whitehorse   145

Winnipeg   147

Yellowknife   152

Conclusion   155

Bibliography   160

Whitehorse

Yellowknife

Gander International

St. John's

Prince George

Edmonton International

Vancouver
International

Kelowna

Calgary
International

Saskatoon /
John G. Diefenbaker

Charlottetown

Moncton

Victoria

Québec / Jean-Lesage
International

Halifax International

Regina

Winnipeg
International

Fredericton

Saint John

Montréal
International
(Mirabel)

Thunder Bay

Sudbury

Montréal
International
(Dorval)

Ottawa
Macdonald-Cartier
International

Toronto
Lester B. Pearson
International

London

National Airports System — Transport Canada

Dedication

For my mother, who had the good sense to give birth to me at the Battle of Britain Hospital, Reading, U.K.

Acknowledgements

A work of this type is only possible with help and support of many people. Without their kindness and assistance, it could not have been completed.

Special thanks go to Robin Smith, the recently retired technical manager of Pearson International Airport. Sylvie Vanburg, also of Pearson, provided me with the photographs of Malton in the late 1930s. Gordon Hamilton, the president of Sypher Mueller, the largest airport consultant firm in Canada, allowed me access to their extensive library.

Bjorn Kristvik of the Royal Norwegian Embassy responded immediately to my entreaty for photos on "Little Norway." The employees of Transport Canada whether in the Maritimes or West were extremely helpful and sent me photographs, brochures and histories of their airports. Angelina Burch of Western Region, Airports was encouraging and located information on the CANOL airports for me. Many employees of Aeroports de Montréal researched and assembled information on Dorval, St. Hubert and Mirabel for me.

Louise Elliott-Edery, Nathalie Hamel and Martine Bagnoud all helped. They even dug through the basements of Mirabel and Dorval Airports in their search for files and photos.

The Airport Managers of several airports responded to my requests for assistance. I am particularly grateful to S.W. Francis (Yarmouth Airport), Robert Barradell (Yellowknife Airport), J.B. MacSween (Hamilton Airport) and Alan Scott (Gander Airport). Nan Taylor of my own MacDonald–Cartier Ottawa Airport allowed me to raid her files, setting a dangerous precedent for future books. The provincial archives were as ever helpful in the extreme. I owe Kelly Nolin (British Columbia), Tim Novak and Nadine Small (Saskatchewan), Marilyn Bell (Prince Edward Island) and Tina Sangris (Northwest Territories) my thanks. At the National Archives here in Ottawa, I relied on several people to sort through the various collections of photos on our aviation heritage.

Dealing with the commercial archives was a sheer pleasure. Canadian Pacific once more came through, as they have with my previous books: Nancy Williatte-Battet deserves special mention, as does Mary Ann Ferguson of Air North. At Air Canada, Carol Gobeil and Brian Loseto provided invaluable assistance. Bombardier Aerospace's Catherine Chase and Gisele Deslaurier were both helpful, but to Garth Dingman, the Supervisor of Photographic Services my gratitude. His photos aptly captured the panoramic beauty of Mirabel and Cartierville airports. Bristol Aerospace of Winnipeg sent me their corporate memory: two volumes on the company's history with photographs of the factory.

In corresponding with all, I was struck by the pride that they displayed in being associated with airports. Again and again, it was mentioned how pleased they were that someone was going to write about "their" airport.

Introduction

The idea for this book began with a letter from my aunt in Australia. Having enjoyed my last book, *Flying Canucks: Famous Canadian Aviators*, she sent me an old photograph taken, she thought, in 1919 on my grandfather's farm at Safrajung outside New Delhi, India.

It showed the unmistakable snout of a World War I Handley Page bomber surrounded by crowds of curious locals. Any aviation enthusiast would know that Handley Page bombers only appeared in the last year of the First World War and primarily over the Western Front. What was one doing in India in 1919? Further research uncovered a fascinating story about how one February morning, my grandfather and the farmworkers saw the giant aircraft — probably the first flying machine they had ever seen — ponderously make for, and land, on one of their sunbaked fields. It had been bought by a local maharajah and flown out to India by two intrepid RAF pilots.

As difficult as piloting an open cockpit Handley Page across the desert was, the journey must have been all the more fraught because outside Europe there were no airfields to land on. The pilots simply looked for vaguely flat places and prayed they wouldn't hit ditches, telegraph lines or fences. Once down, they scrounged gasoline and water and took off again towards the east. My grandfather's farm was to be the last of the impromptu airfields and the crew remained there for weeks, giving joyrides to the locals.

Aviation has come so far in so short a time that we take for granted that airports have always been with us. No doubt, the earliest airports were such farmer's fields or, in Canada, frozen surfaces of lakes. It is hard to imagine that between them and the modern airport, barely a lifetime has passed. Although the airport is very much a phenomenum of the twentieth century there are few old airport buildings in this country still intact. Most were obliterated in the 1940s to put up wartime barracks, and those that survived were buried twenty years later by the glass and steel terminals that symbolized the optimism of the Jet Age. Ocean liners and railway stations can be recycled into floating hotels and boutiques, but the land that airports occupy is too valuable for anything other than industrial estates or housing developments.

In Canada, the earliest airport terminals were simple clapboard affairs, as temporary as the summer cottages that some were. They were utilitarian in design and without the sumptuous art-deco fittings that decorated New York's La Guardia and Paris's Le Bourget. For a young Department of Transport, hardpressed to cope with World War II, there was little to conserve.

When war or peace abandoned them, the airports closed, hangars became derelict, vandalised and then collapsed. The British, with a better sense of history, have preserved both of their earliest airport terminals: Croydon and Hendon, the latter serving as the Royal Air Force's Museum. In the United States, the citizens of Albuquerque, New Mexico and Pueblo, Colorado have made their original airport terminals into local history museums. In Canada, only Edmonton's Blatchford Field and Toronto Island Airport's terminal have been designated as historic sites. In this, the country that President Roosevelt called "The Aerodrome of Democracy," the location of historic airfields such as Harbour Grace, Newfoundland or Leaside, Ontario are known to very few.

This book traces the evolution of airports in Canada. It is neither a technical treatise nor a defense of govern-ment policy. The motives are pure curiousity and nostalgia. It attempts to record our country's immediate past before the present rebuilds it. It explores the sources and history of major airports — the haunts of bushpilots and air aces, tourists and businessmen — and looks at their continuous adaptation to bigger and faster aircraft, and to the govern-ment policies that bankrolled or bankrupted them. Much of the utopian vision that airport planners in the 1930s possessed has been lost to the nervousness of today: terror-ism, environmental pollution, budget deficits and passen-ger congestion. But the airports remain what they were always designed to be: launch pads for the masses, every-man's Cape Canaveral. At once noisy, majestic, cosmopoli-tan and brash — and therein lies their charm.

As to the Handley Page bomber that landed on my grandfather's farm, the maharajah who had bought it or-dered that it be painted pink, the favourite colour, so it was rumoured, of his harem. No sooner had the paint dried than the British government requisitioned the aircraft. The two RAF pilots were ordered to fly it to the Northwest Frontier and frighten some rebellious tribesmen. What they must have thought of the great pink bird that swooped out of the sky is lost to history. The farm at Safrajung became the first airport of New Delhi, and ultimately of India. Perhaps, for me that is where it all began.

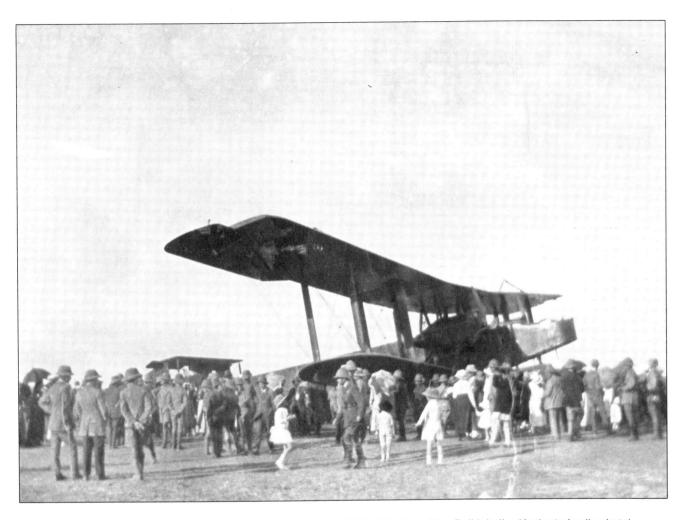

The Handley Page bomber on my grandfather's farm, February 1919, Safrajung, New Delhi, India. (Author's family photo)

Early Days

It is a warm summer's afternoon in Montreal. The year is 1928 and a family has motored over the St. Lawrence bridge to the south shore of the river. Ever since the American aviator Charles Lindbergh flew the Atlantic a year ago, the whole family has become "aviation-mad." Half a century before the concept of theme parks is invented, the family is going to spend the day at one devoted to "The Wonders of Air Travel: St Hubert Airport."

By the time their Packard pulls up to the grass strip at St. Hubert, there are already over a hundred cars parked along the edge of the airfield. The family first gawks at the large billboard at the airport's entrance that proclaims St. Hubert as the headquarters of Canadian Airways Limited. Below the air company's logo is an air route that connects Charlottetown with Vancouver. The father and son in the family no longer call St. Hubert "an air garage." Such pre-war terminology went out with the exploits of Count Jacques De Lesseps and John A.D. McCurdy. They speak of going to the Montreal Airport at St. Hubert.

Everyone is looking forward to seeing aircraft — not the flimsy kite-like contraptions of a decade ago, but powerful, factory-built machines. Nor will the pilots flying them be wrench-carrying inventors or backyard tinkerers, but licensed, leather-jacketed professionals, invariably ex-Royal Flying Corp members. For by 1928, the Atlantic has been conquered, most European capitals are connected by air and aviation is no longer an amusement but touted as the transport of the future.

As the largest city in Canada, it is only proper that Montreal should have an authentic airport such as St. Hubert. Its rivals, Toronto, Vancouver and Winnipeg make do with muddy, grass strips, less airports than airfields. But St. Hubert has put Montreal in the exclusive airport-owning club with the capitals of Europe: London has its Croydon Airport, Paris Le Bourget (where Lindbergh landed) and Berlin Tempelhof. Previously, the family stopped off to picnic at other landing strips on Montreal Island — at LaSalle and Cartierville; but unlike them, St. Hubert has paved runways, two permanent hangars, an administration building, radio station and a meteorological office. Its manager, F.I. Banghart, was himself an airmail pilot with London Air Transport a year earlier.

Long before the Depression would make money for entertainment scarce, watching aircraft land and take-off was a popular way to spend a holiday afternoon. All it required was a car and a picnic basket, and patience. The family is not expecting speciality shops, magazine stalls or even public toilets at St. Hubert. If they see two aircraft taking off that day, they are fortunate. But none of this deters them.

The spectators take their places along the length of the wide apron. The airport's buildings are solidly made and, as the field is already scarred with disused oil drums, airframes and old tires, St. Hubert has a permanent feel to it. The famous airship mooring tower is being built, but as none of the onlookers have ever seen a dirigible (neither have the tower's crew) it is difficult to visualize one tethered to it. To the family, the history that is to unfold at the airport in two years time is unimportant. They are here to watch the planes.

A Fairchild from Rimouski touches down with a roar and staggers past the windsock, up to the hangar. It raises a cloud of dust and the noise its engine makes causes the children to cover their ears. But this is a small price to pay to be able to gawk at the sleek monoplane as it manoeuvres before the hangar. A mechanic, conscious of his audience, rushes up to the plane, careful to avoid the still turning propeller and puts the chocks under the wheels. The pilot looks out of his open cockpit and gives the mechanic the "thumbs up" before turning off the engine.

Then there is a hush, and momentary deafness, as the propeller stops whirling. The pilot eases himself out of the cockpit, removes his leather cap and goggles, revealing a grimy, wind-scarred face. Deafened by the engine, he shouts towards the approaching postmaster, for this is a mail plane. The family notes every move the pilot makes as he alights and walks awkwardly over to the Canadian Airways Ltd. office, unhooking his parachute on the way. The mailbags are unloaded into the awaiting Ford Model T pickup truck, which roars off for the main postal depot in Montreal. The family marvels that yesterday these bags had been aboard a Canadian Pacific steamship far out in the St. Lawrence, and that tomorrow some of their contents will be on their way by air to Toronto and Albany, New York.

After the excitement has died down, a pair of mechanics wheel the aircraft into the hangar. The son points excitedly at another high-wing monoplane taxiing out to take-off on the far side of the field. Everyone cranes their necks in unison to see who owns it; the boy jumping on the Packard's running boards says he can just make out the logo of Colonial Airways. From somewhere in front of the spectator throng, an airport employee, dressed very much like the stationmaster at Windsor Station, calls through a megaphone that the Colonial Airways flight about to take-off is departing Montreal for Albany, with connections to Boston and Hartford. As it too is a mail plane, and carries no passengers, this information is superfluous but at the airport there is a sense of theatre. Besides, the official policy is to encourage what would be called good customer relations. The day might come when the local taxpayer will be asked to foot the bill for the running of the airport.

The pilot waits until given the "go ahead" signal in semaphore by a man with flags and then the aircraft lurches forward to take-off. It clears the fence at the end of the runway and the audience gives a mighty cheer.

Although only mail is carried into St. Hubert, the spectators confidently expect to see passengers deplaning from aircraft by next summer. There is speculation that one of the giant Ford Trimotors (currently featured on bubblegum cards) will be used on the cross-border run. The Trimotors can carry up to twelve passengers in comfort and, according to the newsreels, are even now being used by Northwest Airlines to fly from Pembina, North Dakota to Winnipeg, Manitoba.

The airfield has grown quiet and no other flights are expected before sunset. Picnic baskets are opened, and the whole family sit on the grass or the Packard's running boards. After their meal, the children rush off to a pair of clapboard cabins that share a large sign proclaiming "Aviation Postcard". In one, tickets for aerial joyrides can be had and at the other, snacks, postcards and cigarettes are sold. Although no one knows it, these dusty shacks are the forerunners of the glamorous shopping complexes that will engulf airports half a century later.

Later, accompanied by their parents, the children watch the weatherman, or meteorological officer, go about his business. He takes and records the readings of various instruments: barometers, thermometers, wind direction and speed. To the delight of all assembled, he sends up a small hydrogen balloon and, using his stopwatch and theodolite, takes observations on the location of the balloon every minute. This enables him, the boy tells his sister, to figure out the wind's velocity at various elevations above the earth.

At sunset, St. Hubert's lights come on, each with a meaning. The white boundary lights mark the edge of the airport; the green lights the runways; and the red lights on

St. Hubert, August 1930. With its cavernous hangar and concrete apron, the airport was far in advance of any other in the country. The cause of all the excitement, the R-100 can be seen moored after its Atlantic crossing. (Pratt & Whitney Archives)

top of the buildings and telegraph poles – the danger for incoming aircraft. There is even, although only visible if one stands on the roof of the family sedan, an illuminated wind-direction indicator at the far side of the airport. This gives a pilot the best direction and runway for landing.

Whatever aircraft is due to land that night, the family never finds out for it's time to return home. They will be back soon, the father promises, to watch a giant airship arrive at St. Hubert, non-stop across the Atlantic from England.

The History of Airports in Canada

Long before there were airports there were landing fields. Even before the Air Age had begun, men launched gas filled balloons into the sky over Canada. The first recorded instance took place in Montreal on 15 October 1834, when advertisements in the newspapers announced there would be an exhibition of Montgolfier balloons at the Champ de Mars parade ground. Three small balloons were to be sent up and all proceeds would be shared between the Montreal General Hospital and the Orphan Asylum. Unfortunately, the event was rescheduled because of the "unruliness of the crowd" and there is no record of when this occurred.

The inhabitants of Upper Canada saw their first balloon in rather different circumstances. On 18 May 1835, a paper hot air balloon was sent up in the yard of the Farmer's Hotel in Kingston. As a local newspaper ferreted out, the event was far from being in the cause of science. A travelling troupe of comedians had been imprisoned for debt and hoped to raise bail money in this way. The reporter dryly commented that the results were sadly disappointing– not for science, but for the comedians.

By the 1850s, a number of local aeronauts had launched themselves into the skies in balloons from fields and fair grounds. The most memorable of these took place on 21 June 1879, when Montrealers Charles Page, Professor Grimley and James Creelman ascended in a balloon from the Shamrock Lacrosse Grounds in Westmount. Although they travelled as far as St. Hyacinthe, forty-five miles (72 kilometres) from Montreal, nothing came of the flight and the lacrosse grounds were forgotten as the first known launch pad for aerial travel in Canada.

However, balloons, whether in ascent or descent, required little land and their heyday occurred before telegraph wires and hydroelectric pylons were strung across the countryside. The first airports everywhere in the world were undoubtedly the open field in front of the aircraft inventor's barn. Few early aviators were as fortunate as Orville and Wilbur Wright, to be able to use the unlimited sands

The origins of every airport in Canada can be traced to the frozen lake at Baddeck Bay, Cape Breton, Nova Scotia, where on 23 February, 1909, John Alexander Douglas McCurdy flew the *Silver Dart*. (National Archives of Canada RE 64-2262)

The first landing grounds were usually farmers fields. This, the main airfield of PEI in the 1920s, was part of Jack and Louise Jenkins' farm at Upton. (PEI Public Archives 3523/61)

of Kittyhawk, North Carolina for experimentation. So short was the range of early flying machines (and so unreliable their engines) that the pilot usually had no choice but to alight where ever he could. He simply looked for the nearest open stretch of land, hoped it was devoid of fences or ditches, and aimed for it. Before 1914, the number of available landing fields were so few that American aviation pioneer Glenn Curtiss wrote he was sure marine flying would develop quicker than land, because landing fields were not needed by seaplanes and the surface of the water already provided for smooth runways.

Canada has lakes and rivers in abundance and it was inevitable that the first flight would take place off one. On 23 February 1909, John Alexander Douglas McCurdy flew a pusher biplane, the *Silver Dart*, off the smooth ice on frozen Bras d'Or Lake at Baddeck Bay, Nova Scotia. But McCurdy could not avoid landing fields indefinitely. That summer, to obtain funding from the military for further development, he was forced to demonstrate his fragile aircraft at an army camp in Petawawa, Ontario. As he had feared, landing on the parade ground completely wrecked the *Silver Dart* and with it his chances of government assistance.

In the summer of 1910, great aerial exhibitions took place in the suburbs of Montreal and Toronto. Both were on fields rented from local farmers. The land was levelled, fences were taken down and bleachers were provided for a paying audience. The aviators must have enjoyed the smooth landings that the prepared fields provided, for they knew that these were exceptional circumstances. At the end of the meets, the pilots returned to their gypsy lives of constantly looking out for convenient places to land and take-off from — usually parks, race tracks, exhibition grounds.

Pre-World War I aircraft could best be described as a cross between motorized box-kites and bird cages with wings. Their pilots had little control over where they landed as their cockpits were filled with complicated instruments that required all their attention. Just keeping directional and lateral stability during flight was a constant struggle. Managing all the wheels and levers that controlled the rudder, the wingwarping and the petrol pump meant that the pilot had his hands full.

However, he was wise to keep an eye on the ground as he skimmed over it. Without an altimeter and airspeed indicator, landing required a fair measure of skill and judgement. Worse, the early undercarriages were made of metal tubes that collapsed if anything other than a three-point landing was attempted. The field chosen had to be as smooth as possible and pre-World War I pilots quickly learnt to recognise what they called an "aerial garage." As a result, the first airfield in most Canadian cities was the local golf course (Ottawa), race track (Vancouver), suburban park (Calgary), polo grounds (Montreal) or a disused target practice range (Toronto).

In 1915, the United States government published a list of fields where aviators had a reasonable chance of setting down, or taking-off, without killing themselves. It makes astonishing reading. The list includes baseball fields, dry riverbeds, country clubs and even graveyards (one must assume that these were actually memorial gardens, rather

The Curtiss Flying School built the first permanent airfield in 1915, at Long Branch, outside Toronto. (National Archives of Canada PA 61493)

than tombstone-dotted death traps). Having just paid for the infrastructure of the Railway Age, both the United States and the Canadian governments saw little need to purchase myriad properties for airfields. Besides, few taxpayers actually flew, and the aircraft had not proved itself to be more than a curiosity, or an expensive amusement.

It was only during the First World War that the municipalities realized a permanent space for aviation had to be allocated. No one could have guessed the aircraft would play such a decisive part in the conflict. Within a year of the start of hostilities, the day of the amateur flying machine tinkerer had ended, and aircraft were being mass-produced much like Mr. Ford's Model Ts. With the average life expectancy over the Western Front being about two weeks, the numbers of young men that had to be taught to fly was on a scale unimaginable in 1913.

In Canada, having failed to convince Ottawa to create its own air arm (and buy his aircraft), J.A.D. McCurdy became a director in the American Curtiss Aeroplane & Motor Company. Canada had entered the First World War without its own air force, and McCurdy seized the opportunity to open a flying school to train Canadian pilots for the Royal Flying Corps (RFC). The Curtiss Company built the first permanent airfield in Canadian history at Long Branch, outside Toronto. In 1917, as the carnage in aerial warfare began to take its toll, the British government began a massive training program for the Royal Flying Corps in Canada. The Dominion was seen by the War Office as ideal for training pilots as it was sufficiently far away from the Front, had unlimited space, and was close to American industry and cities. Although the airfields the RFC built were for military purposes, they set the pattern for future commercial airports in Canada.

The First World War was a watershed for aviation in Canada. As it would in the Second World War, Canada provided extensive training and patrol facilities for its allies. In return, when the RFC and the United States Navy left their Canadian bases to return home, they presented their hosts with fighter planes, flying boats, air harbours and airfields. By Armistice Day 1918, the Dominion found itself in possession of six aerodromes, as they were called – all in Ontario – and two air harbours on the Atlantic coast.

In the optimism of the Roaring Twenties, everyone realized that aircraft that had been designed to bomb far behind the enemy lines during the war, also had the potential of delivering mail and medicine across vast stretches of Canada. Unlike railroads, or steamships, they required little investment and were exciting to operate. Like most of the industrialized world, Canadians became aviation-mad.

During the hostilities more than 8,000 Curtiss JN-4 training aircraft were built, mainly in Toronto. In 1919, most were declared surplus to military requirements and auctioned off for a pittance. What had been a rich man's toy before the war now came within reach of anyone who had $50. Another by-product of the conflict were the hundreds of young pilots, now unemployed, that the RFC flying schools had been churning out. The combination of both factors would change aviation in Canada forever.

In Oshawa, Ontario, Armistice Day was celebrated by an exuberant officer from the local RFC unit who flew his plane down the main street, and clipped off all the flagpoles with the wheels of the undercarriage. Doing aerobatics, or

Canada has lakes and rivers in abudance and there seemed in the 1920s little need to build airports. The greater part of early transcontinental flights were made by flying boats like this Vickers Vedette. (National Archives of Canada RE 69-2895)

stunting, over a girlfriend's house was another temptation for a pilot. In the Toronto area, one of the favourite games for the barnstormers was to wait for the Barrie express train and then fly low over it, bumping the roof of the carriages with their undercarriage. For a finale, the pilot would dip down in front of the locomotive, almost on the tracks, keeping just ahead of the cowcatcher. The idea was to stay sufficiently far from the engine driver and passengers so the identifying numbers on the tail of the aircraft could not be seen. The skies over North America soon filled with air races, air charter companies, parachute jumpers and wing walkers.

It was apparent that what had, five years before, been an Edwardian gentleman's hobby had degenerated into an aerial free-for-all, typical of the Jazz Age, with cowboy-pilots performing hair-raising stunts over urban areas.

As aircraft crashes multiplied, newspapers and staid citizens began to call for some sort of law to control a sport that had gotten out of hand. But it was the Canadian Pacific Railway that saw the possibilities of commercial aviation, and it prompted the federal government to decide on some form of legislation. On 6 June 1919, to control civil aviation in Canada, Parliament passed the Air Board Act.

Through it, the government could regulate commercial air routes and license airports. It would undertake some aerial forestry protection and even mount exploration flights to the far north. It would also license and inspect airports and air harbours. But the onus to build and operate these facilities was very much on local communities and private businesses. Having just fought an expensive war, the Dominion had neither the money nor the political will to finance an airport for every town that wanted one.

In contrast to Ottawa's policies in the aftermath of the Second World War, the Air Board was very much a low key, low budget affair. The Department of National Defence,

The actual requirements for an airfield were modest: a plot of land free of tree stumps, with the ditches filled in and a windsock. This is McLelland Field, Saskatoon, Saskatchewan, July 1920. (Saskatchewan Archives Board R-A9578-1)

using the aircraft given by Britain and the United States, maintained two flying schools at Camp Borden and Rockliffe, Ontario. An aerial survey unit was also funded at Morley, Alberta, on the eastern slope of the Rockies, for forest fire protection. But these initiatives were the limit of federal involvement in aviation. Flying was still a fringe form of travel, and there seemed little need to spend money on clearing and levelling land for airports, when the many lakes and rivers in Canada provided free air harbours in summer and frozen landing fields in the winter.

Despite this official apathy, airfields began to appear throughout the country. Some were private, for use by a local flying club or an aircraft manufacturer or for a specific purpose. One of the stranger airports was near Saskatoon, Saskatchewan. In 1920, a Chinese company, Keng Wah Aviation, opened a flying school north of the city to train pilots from China and the United States for Dr. Sun Yat Sen's army. Other airports were public, used by barnstormers and mail carriers who paid landing fees, and served as ports of entry from the United States. But whether private or public, only an Air Board inspector could license an airfield.

There were also air harbours on each coast, and at a few places (like Rockcliffe, Ontario and Rimouski, Quebec) facilities for both. The first air harbour license was awarded to Laurentide Air Services at Lac à la Tortue near Grand'Mére, Quebec. The Aerial Service Company at Regina received Airfield Licence No. 1. The 1922 Report of the Air Board listed thirty-six airfield/air harbours in Canada, with only seven belonging to the government.

The requirements for an actual airfield were very modest. On the average, it was a plot of land, free of tree stumps and fences, about ninety acres in size. The runways were laid out in either large crosses or T-shapes, and about 2,500 to 3,000 feet (762 to 914 metres) in length. They were

AIRCRAFT AT UPTON P.E.I. Feb 32.

The scene at Upton Airport, Charlottetown, Prince Edward Island, 1932, best conveys the simplicity of early airports. Note the gas pumps by the car. (National Archives of Canada PA 126628)

arranged so that the aircraft could land, or take-off, directly into the prevailing wind. There might have been some artificial drainage, and all the ditches and potholes had been filled up to the level of the field. Readily available materials, usually gravel or cinders, were used to surface the most used portions of the runway. Gasoline and tools might be stored in a canvas hangar, or a barn, at one end of the field. A location marker, a windsock and possibly a telephone completed the technical requirements. If they were fortunate, the pilots and ground crew sheltered in the farm house that had come with the sale of the property. There was no lighting, no air traffic control, no weather bulletins and no passengers to worry about.

It suited the aviation-mad pilot in his goggles and riding jodhpurs. Once airborne, he navigated by dead reckoning, taking bearings on known objects to confirm his position.

The airport he had left, and the airport he was flying toward, had no control over him, or even knew where he was. The situation had changed little from the days of the sailing ships, whose locations remained unknown until they actually arrived in port.

Air harbours required only a slipway and a stretch of water that didn't have to be particularly deep. For the seaplane of the 1920s, four feet (1.2 metres) was sufficient to provide draft.

In rural Canada, an airfield was a private venture. At Charlottetown, for example, Dr. Jack Jenkins, the chief physician at the local hospital, made a field on his horse stud farm available for aircraft to land on. He and his wife, Louise, took flying lessons and bought their own red Puss Moth: registered CF-PEI. Because of their enthusiasm, Upton Field became Prince Edward Island's first airport.[1]

1. For the story of Louise Jenkins, and other women aviators, I am indebted to Joyce Spring's book, *Daring Lady Flyers*, Pottersfield Press, 1994.

The Flying Club Scheme

It was this love of flying that penny-pinching governments tapped to create the earliest airports. In post-war Britain, a nucleus for an air force had been kept alive by encouraging local flying clubs and universities to operate their own air squadrons. In 1927, Ottawa decided to implement the same plan in Canada. The Department of National Defence realized that in case of war, the tiny permanent air force could never meet even the most basic of strategic needs. Since the demobilization of 1918, it was short both of pilots and airports. To overcome the lack of trained pilots, between 1925-28 the RCAF even began recruiting in Britain. Now, by fostering a network of flying clubs across Canada, Ottawa was assured that, should they ever be needed, it would have available airports with a pool of trained pilots.

Of historic importance to the development of Canadian aviation, Order-in-Council P.C. 1878 stated that a group of aircraft enthusiasts, anywhere in the country, would receive official encouragement and financial assistance to begin and run a flying club. For its part the club had to maintain its aerodrome, erect a hangar, employ an instructor and a mechanic, and, at any one time, be teaching thirty of its members to fly. If these conditions were met, the government would provide it with two aircraft and $100 for each member that successfully obtained a licence.

It was a scheme that suited everyone. Cities like Hamilton, Ontario were quick to realize a government-sponsored flying club could also be used as a municipal airport, and applied immediately for aid. To enthusiastic young men and women in Toronto, Victoria, Saskatoon and Moose Jaw, the token money and the war-surplus Avros were all the encouragement they needed. As the government had hoped, the Flying Club Scheme was an immediate success: by 1929, there were twenty-four clubs with their own airfields across the country. As the local communities had hoped, out of the club property came the first municipal airports. During World War II, the flying clubs repaid Ottawa's investment by training thousands of Allied aircrew in the British Commonwealth Air Training Plan (BCATP).

Airmail Routes

The military apart, Ottawa had its own agenda for encouraging flying clubs across the country. Besides becoming the local airport, the flying clubs aerodromes fitted in well with the Post Office's proposed airmail service. Although the first airmail flights in Canada had taken place between Toronto, Ottawa and Montreal as early as 1918 these had been performed by bored Royal Air Force pilots as little more than experiments or "stunts."

Given the vast distances between urban centres in Canada and the limited range aircraft of the day possessed, it was a brave politician that even suggested the setting up of a national airmail system. It was also thought that the transportation system in sparsely populated Canada was already over-developed with an abundance of railways, canals and harbours. But the Canadian postal authorities and the public had watched enviously the success of subsidised airmail in the United States and Europe and felt that they too were entitled to the same service.

Below the border, the U.S. Post Office had lobbied for federal appropriations for airmail as early as 1911. As a result, the first regular airmail route between New York and Washington D.C. began in 1918. Barely two years later, service was inaugurated between New York and San Francisco. By 1927, when Charles Lindbergh, one of the U.S. Post Office airmail pilots, flew the Atlantic, there was already a well developed network of airports, navigation aids and aircraft industry.

In Canada, throughout the 1920s, many communities continued to remain isolated through the long winter. The Magdalen Islands were, even then, dependant from December to April on their mail being floated out in barrels and picked up off Prince Edward Island. The scattered villages on the River and Gulf of St. Lawrence were similarly cut off most of the winter, and received their mail by dog team every six weeks. The advantage of airmail to these and many hundreds of other outlying communities was obvious.

Prime Minister Mackenzie King must have seized the Post Office's lobbying for a federally financed airmail system as a godsend. In 1926, at the Imperial Conference in London, King had rashly committed Canada to building an airship terminal. It was to be part of an imperial communications system of dirigible routes that would, it was thought, draw the British Empire closer together. Montreal was the logical choice for such a base, but when the city refused to be drawn in the federal government was forced to finance the project by itself. If the proposed airship facility could also be made to serve as an airmail terminal, the expense might be justified. The British airship survey team sent out to Canada chose the village of St. Hubert, outside Montreal for their airport, and it also became the first link in a national airmail service.

If the Atlantic Ocean could not be conquered, at least ships could be met as far out as possible and the mail taken off them and flown to St. Hubert. When the actual transfer on the high seas proved more difficult than imagined, the mail was brought by the pilot boat to Rimouski and then flown from an airfield at the pier. Thus both St. Hubert and Rimouski became the first government-built and operated airports in Canada. Airmail contracts were awarded to Canadian Colonial Airways, Canadian Airways and Western Canada Airways to carry the mail between Rimouski and St. Hubert, and then from there to link up with the American system at Albany, New York. Contracts were also given to fly mail between Toronto and Ottawa and in Western Canada.

The Canadian air companies used lumbering Fokkers and smaller Boeing 40Bs. Both had accommodations for passengers as well as mail bags; the Fokkers could carry eight passengers and the little Boeings four. Typically, the pilot sat in an open cockpit away from the mail bags and passengers. The Post Office was so afraid their property might be tampered with inflight, they first tried to bar passengers entirely, later only agreeing if the mail bags could be locked in the toilet at the rear of the cabin.

However, it was the effect of these intrepid travellers using airfields that would change them from muddy pastures to "air depots." With a commercial market to compete for, air companies were forced to tear down the barns that had come with the property, and replace them with two-storey buildings that had waiting rooms, toilets and heating. The local hash-slinging diner, or rural tavern, that had been good enough for the pilots and mechanics, was also forced to improve its cuisine or go out of business.

With their experience in luxury trains and ocean liners, the Europeans were far ahead in passenger comfort at an airport. By 1927, flying between such closely situated cities as Amsterdam, Brussels, London and Paris was no longer a novelty but a convenience. In an amazing display of equanimity, all European states agreed to facilitate the examination of passengers, and their luggage, at ports of entry. North American tourists would write home that when they flew Imperial Airways from London, there was no rude awakening in the very early hours for the inspection of passports or luggage as there were on trains. The paved walkways in front of the arrival and departure buildings at Le Bourget (Paris), Templehof (Berlin) and Croydon (London) eliminated the dust and slush that passengers had to put up with at Canadian airports. Sitting in a cold Western Canada Airways aircraft, in shoes and clothes muddied and wet from the puddles on the airfield was enough to discourage anyone from ever travelling by air again.

In the United States too, there was already a defined form of airport architecture. Architects felt that apprehensive passengers might be reassured with the familiar solidity of a mini-Grand Central as an airport terminal. Sometimes the only differences between railway and air terminals was in the choice of furniture. Contemporary photographs of American airport interiors show a preponderance of wicker furniture. No doubt this was to get the passenger accustomed to it, as the seats on board the aircraft were wicker as well. The other peculiarity at an air terminal, whether America, European or Canadian, was a weighing scale for passengers. As embarrassing as this might have been, all about to board the aircraft were carefully weighed and the total weight computed against the prevailing wind and the aircraft's capabilities. Except for St. Hubert Airport, it would be another decade before airports in Canada came even close to their American and European counterparts.

However, to be competitive with the railways, mail had to be delivered by air overnight. Until the electrification of rural Canada in the 1940s, there was little to guide a pilot across the country after dark. All he could hope for was that sympathetic farmers would light bonfires along the route, or that he could follow car and locomotive headlights that might be going in his direction. If it was difficult to find a proper landing field during the day, putting down after dark, skipping over barbed-wire fences, telephone lines and ditches, was suicidal.

After sunset, the only means by which an airport manager could communicate with a pilot was by either using flares or a hand-held searchlight. He flashed the light (which had removable coloured filters) at the aircraft or fired a flare from a Very pistol[2] to authorize take-offs and landings. On the ground, as in the air, it was the pilot's responsibility to watch out for other aircraft. Influenced no doubt by the traditional "keep right" rule of the sea, the pilot kept right of traffic.[3]

By 1927, a major city airport at night might boast a row of wavering oil flares to mark the landing path, and a lighted cone that showed wind direction. The smoky flares became the airmail pilot's only points of reference as he tried to gain some perspective for judging the angle of approach prior to touchdown. Kept ready at great cost, the flare pots were seen as more morale-boosters than practical.

---

2. This was a coloured flare, fired from a large bore pistol named after its inventor. Pilots and ground staff used them to warn each other.

3. It explains why, even today, the captain of a 747 will choose to sit on the left.

The pilots complained that in bad weather, when the flares were desperately needed, they could not be seen anyway. At smaller airfields there was no one on duty after dark, and the pilot landed unaided, tied the aircraft down himself and walked into town.

Whatever the problems, commercial aviation caught on in Canada. Statistics demonstrate that aircraft, air travel and airports had become part of a viable and dependable transportation system. From 1921 to 1931 mail and cargo shipments increased more than thirty times, going from 79,200 pounds (36,000 kilograms) in 1921 to 2.86 million pounds (1.3 million kilograms) in 1931. What is more astounding, given the capacity of the aircraft at the time, passenger travel had also soared, going from under 10,000 in 1921 to 100,000 in 1931.[4]

The Trans-Canada Airway

Although the airmail system was proving to be a success, by 1928 it was becoming more and more evident that if Canadians were not going to invest in the infrastructure for a viable air transportation system in their own country, the Americans would. Passenger-carrying airlines had long been heavily subsidized in Europe, both as status symbols and as instruments of government policy, but Ottawa's interest in aviation had so far been niggardly.

Fortunately, the Controller of Civil Aviation at this time was the strong-minded John Armistead Wilson. It was his vision and determination that would radically alter government policy. Canada, Wilson wrote, as a great trading nation, could not afford to ignore the new form of travel and had to move with the times. The cost of establishing an "Airway" from coast to coast with airports, communications and emergency fields was estimated to be between $5 and $6 million. But, he warned, American transport companies were waiting to tap into the traffic at the main population centres in Canada, all of which lay along the national boundary, and feed it into the American airway system.[5]

4. Statistics Canada. *Aviation in Canada.* Ottawa. Ministry of Supply & Services, 1986, p.37.

5. J.A. Wilson "Aviation in Canada" *The Journal of the Engineering Institute of Canada*, Toronto: March 1937, reprinted 1986 pg. 7.

As the railway builders of the previous century had known, an appeal to national sovereignty never failed to elicit public support and, in 1928, permission was given to begin a survey for a Trans-Canada Airway. The Liberal government of Mackenzie King, which until now operated only the airports at St. Hubert and Rimouski, tentatively agreed to building a chain of airfields from Halifax to Vancouver. For each town or city that wanted an airport, the Department of National Defence, which had jurisdiction over civil aviation, offered to put up half the cost of runway lighting, and match the municipality's contribution with a grant of up to $10,000. It proved to be an inexpensive gesture for the federal government, as with the onslaught of the Depression few municipalities could meet their committment.

Inter-city mails and passenger traffic dropped off when the Depression brought industry to a standstill. In 1930 the Liberals lost the election to the Conservatives and all airmail contracts were cancelled. In a memorable quote, the new Prime Minister R.B. Bennett said that with 300,000 Canadians on relief there was little need for a government-subsidised mail plane to fly over them nightly. The half-finished network of airfields would have been effectively orphaned, had not the difficult economic times

In 1928, the Controller for Civil Aviation was John Armistead Wilson. It was primarily his vision and determination that made the airports of the Trans-Canada Airway possible. (National Archives of Canada PL 117438)

made a huge labour force of unemployed men suddenly available.

In 1935, Bennett's Conservative government was defeated, having lost due to the massive unemployment across the country and a drought that had reduced the prairies to airborne dust. Mackenzie King's Liberals swept back into power, and proved to be the most aviation-minded government the country has seen.

King, or more precisely his Minister of Harbours and Railways Clarence Decatur Howe, took civil aviation away from the military and put it into the newly created Department of Transport. By thus giving it a permanent godfather, Howe elevated commercial aviation to the same level in the aegis of the national transportation industry as the mighty railways. J.A. Wilson's hopes of the government fully committing itself to the building and operating of airports from coast to coast now seemed within reach. For once, Canada was ahead of the United States. Not before 1940 was US federal aid for airports allowed, and it was left to local government and the private sector to put up terminals and runways through the Depression.

The 1930s were a decade that fostered men of iron principles and determination — Joseph Stalin, Winston Churchill and John Foster Dulles were representative of their era — and aviation in Canada was fortunate to have one such individual. Not only was the first Minister of Transport, C.D. Howe, responsible for the introduction of the Act to create the Department of Transport, but in 1937 he also bulldozed through Parliament the Trans-Canada Airlines Act. The operation of a national airway and airline, and later the creation of a judicial body to handle the licensing of air routes, were to a large extent the brainchildren of this American immigrant.

Fortunately, the massive unemployment relief projects that the Depression had spawned coincided with the laying out of airfields across the most difficult section in all of Canada: between Cochrane, Ontario and the Manitoba border. The Department of Transport surveyors had estimated that, for the safe passage of transcontinetal aircraft, at least twenty-seven airfields had to be carved out across this particular wilderness. Even today, the names of those airfields — Nagogami, Ogahalla, Wagaming, Nakina — echo more of the Northwest Campaign of 1885 than the Air Age.

Through the relief scheme, large numbers of single men, made homeless because of hard times, were sent to remote areas of the bush and gathered in camps along the route. There they cleared forests, drained the muskeg and hacked roads and runways out of virtually unexplored territory. Because costs were to be kept at a minimum, the equipment used were teams of horses, wheelbarrows and dynamite. The workers endured plagues of blackflies in the summer, and below-zero temperatures in the winter, to be paid $1 a day. If the airfield required a caretaker to look after the runway and perimeter lights, power lines had to be brought in or a generator installed.

Between 1932-36, a total of fifty airports were constructed at hundred mile (161 kilometre) intervals, with emergency landing fields every fifty miles (81 kilometres). By early 1938, all ninety-four airfields of the Trans-Canada Airway from Montreal to Vancouver were nearing completion, and scheduled coast-to-coast air service was begun on 6 March. At every hundred miles or so across Canada there was now a fully-equipped airport with, if necessary, three runways 3000 feet by 300 feet (914 metres by 91 metres) in size, boundary lighting, a radio beacon and a teletype machine. Some of the airports built during the Depression, like Vancouver's and Edmonton's, would prosper and become the mini-cities they are today; others, like St. Eugene, Quebec, Ramore, Ontario and Whitemouth, Manitoba, served their purpose and were slowly relegated by technology to the backwaters of airport development. But in 1938 no country of comparable size (not the Soviet Union, not Australia) could boast such an accomplishment.

The knowledge gained by the Civil Aviation Branch in airport construction between 1928-38 would be well used during the Second World War, when the hundreds of airbases were required for training, patrolling and ferrying. The epic construction of the Airway, a feat unknown to most Canadians, can be compared with the building of the Canadian Pacific Railway a generation earlier or the Distant Early Warning (DEW) Line two decades later.

In addition to financing the remote airfields, federal funds were also available for municipal airports in the major urban areas. Toronto, which had long shied away from building its own airport, now received funding for two: at Malton and at Toronto Island. Ottawa City Council, which had also refused to invest in its own airport, now saw Uplands completed. Runways were hard-surfaced at Vancouver, Lethbridge and Edmonton. At St. Hubert, the original airport of Canada, a radio range and the first control tower in the country was built. Symbolically, the old airship mooring mast was demolished at the same time. The imperial dream of binding the colonies by airship had died after the Airship R-100's single successful trip to Canada.

With the increasing use of all-metal airliners, such as the DC-2 and the Boeing 247, runways had to be lengthened and hardstanding became necessary. Grass turf that had been sufficient for the wood and wire Jennies could not support a 12,000 pound (5,400 kilogram) aircraft, especially in the slush of melting snow.

Communications began to play a major role. Until now, when an aircraft took-off, no communication was possible with it until it actually landed somewhere. There was no method of monitoring its progress, and its arrival at the intended destination must have been a relief for all concerned. By 1935 most airports were connected by either teletype or telephone to warn of an aircraft's expected arrival. Some form of air traffic control and two-way radio was becoming necessary as the number of aircraft in the sky increased. The old "see and be seen" dictum did not work in areas of low visibility, or with the faster aircraft now coming into service. In North America, the "airways" (fixed routes between navigation facilities) were established and all aircraft were required to fly along them. Vertical separation was assured by the air traffic controller assigning aircraft to a series of fixed altitudes known as levels. A pilot filed a flight plan, detailing where he was to go and when, and reported his position along the route. Air traffic controllers could then radio him to adjust his position to avoid other aircraft.

These early technical innovations had a major impact on airports as it changed their role from that of mere landing fields to one of controlling the whole flight. With the use of radar after the war, this control increased even more as the air traffic controller no longer had to rely on the pilot radioing in his position. Through radar coverage he knew the location of all aircraft within his area.

Trans-Atlantic Airports and Air Harbours

Not yet part of Canada, Newfoundland was the nearest landfall to Europe and had been associated with trans-oceanic flights since 1919. When *The Daily Mail*, a British newspaper, offered a prize of £10,000 for the first successful trans-Atlantic flight, outlying farms on the island became impromptu airfields for several of the competitors. On 14 June 1919, British aviators John Alcock and Arthur Whitton Brown took off from Lester's Field, west of the city of St. John's, to make for Europe. So their Vickers Vimy could lift off with a full load of gasoline, local volunteers worked for four days to remove tree stumps and rocks and fill in the ditches unknowingly creating Newfoundland's first airport. Sixteen hours and twenty-eight minutes later, Alcock and Brown landed in a bog in Clifden, Ireland, having bridged the Atlantic Ocean successfully.[6]

Through the years, Newfoundland continued to be the jumping off point for Atlantic fliers. On 16 May 1919, three US Navy flying boats stopped at the temporary air harbour of Trepassey Bay, south of St. John's, on their way across the ocean. Amelia Earhart would also use Trepassy in her record-breaking flight to Wales on 18 June 1928.

Of all the Newfoundland airfields used to cross the Atlantic, the two at Harbour Grace deserve a special place in aviation history. The first had been cleared by locals for Vice-Admiral Sir Mark Kerr, an unsuccessful competitor of Alcock and Brown. It was succeeded by a second airfield that, for the decade between 1927-37, was the jumping off point for long-distance fliers from around the world — Americans, Australians, Hungarians, Poles and Canadians— all attempting to fly further across the Atlantic than the other. From Harbour Grace on 9 October, 1930, Montreal pilot Erroll Boyd and his navigator Harry P. Conner took off for Croydon, England in a used Bellanca, patriotically called *The Maple Leaf*. Although a broken fuel line forced them down twenty-four hours later on a beach in the Scilly Isles, they were the first Canadians to fly the Atlantic.

By 1937, aviation technology had sufficiently advanced so that the commercial airlines could plan on flying the Atlantic for profit. Britain's Imperial Airways chose the sheltered Newfoundland harbour of Botwood for their flying boat service. Later, in expectation of long-range land-planes, the British government would build a huge airport at Gander. Not to be outdone, Imperial Airway's American competitor, Pan American Airways put up a mooring sta-

---

6. Momuments in Ireland and Newfoundland commerate the flight; the Newfoundland one is located at Blackmarsh Road, St. John's.

Vice Admiral Sir Mark Kerr test-flying his Handley Page aircraft at Harbour Grace, Newfoundland on 10 June 1919. Four days before he was to leave, Alcock and Brown successfully flew the Atlantic Ocean from a nearby airfield. (National Archives of Canada PA 121926)

tion at Shediac, New Brunswick for its trans-Atlantic service from New York to Southampton.

Even during the Second World War, both Botwood and Shediac were part of a regular flying boat service operated either by the British Overseas Airways Corporation (BOAC, the successor to Imperial Airways) or Pan American. When, on 24 October 1945, the last Pan American "Clipper" took off from Botwood on its 455th flight, it brought to an end the romantic flying boat era for Newfoundland and Canada.

Airports and the Second World War

Unlike the First World War, Canada entered the Second with an Air Force, a Department of Transport and, thanks to the Trans-Canada Airway, a viable system for pilots to cross the country without venturing into the United States. The newly built airports would be increasingly in demand for wartime projects like the British Commonwealth Air Training Plan (BCATP), the Atlantic Ferry Service and the Northwest Staging Route. In 1940, the Minister of Transport C.D. Howe was made Minister for Munitions and Supply.[7] So essential did he consider the construction and operation of more airports to the war machine, that he took over all responsibility for them from the Department of Transport for the duration.

Between 1939-45, on his instructions (sometimes personally supervised) acres of blueprints were scanned, tons of concrete were poured onto runways and truckloads of planks hammered into hangars. Across Canada, Depression-battered communities like Assiniboia Saskatchewan, Neepawa Alberta, and Dunville Ontario, discovered that the construction of the BCTAP airports provided their first

real prosperity since 1929. All the manual labour used to build the runways, erect the control towers and barracks was local. The money the men and women earned at the airport flowed back to the local shopowners, real estate agents, boarding houses, taverns and barber shops. From a thin chain of airmail airfields a decade before, Canada had transformed itself into, as President Roosevelt described it, "The Aerodrome of Democracy."

When Hitler invaded Poland in 1939, few airports in Canada were immediately suited for military operations. Runways built to stand the impact of DC-3s at 4,000 pounds (1,800 kilograms) could not take the pounding of the four-engined Flying Fortresses and Liberators soon to come. Airport managers, who might have seen five take-offs and landings a day, now watched in bewilderment from new control towers as a continuous stream of "Yellow Perils" (training aircraft) bobbed over their domain at all heights, piloted by grim-faced students struggling with the controls. Pre-war airport personnel barely had time to adapt to camouflage nets, anti-aircraft batteries and rows of barracks before the introduction of female pilots and mechanics into a hitherto all male preserve!

Even as war was declared, delegates from the British government and the other Dominions were meeting in Ottawa to ask for assistance in training their pilots. Starved

---

7. By 1940, the hard-driving Clarence Decatur Howe had his finger in so many pies he was called "The Minister for Nearly Everything."

Canada was dotted with hundreds of training schools throughout the war, earning the title "The Aerodrome of Democracy." This one is in Muskoka, Ontario, 1942. (Royal Norwegian Embassy, Ottawa)

Dorval Airport was built in 1941 to take over the ferrying of aircraft to England from over-crowded St. Hubert. (Aeroport de Montréal Archives)

between the wars, the RCAF had few enough airbases itself, and the government was hard pressed to know where to teach the eager young airmen, soon to be pouring into Canada to learn to fly. At first, sixty-four flying training schools were envisaged, but by 1941, with airpower playing an ever increasing part in all military theatres, this was increased to seventy-five. Besides building more airfields,

the Department of Transport decided to take over the municipal airports in the Dominion, staffing and equipping them for their new roles. Ultimately, by the final years of the BCATP, 149 new airports had been built and seventy-three existing ones expanded.

Other established airports were requisitioned and developed because of their strategic locations. St. Hubert and Dorval outside Montreal were the assembly points for the vital Atlantic Ferry to England. With the German successes in Europe there was a legitimate fear that the British Colony of Newfoundland might be overrun and the RCAF assumed protection of the vast airport at Gander. When the United States entered the war, Edmonton and Whitehorse became major refuelling points on the Northwest Staging Route to supply aircraft to the Soviet Union. Inevitably, after the Japanese attack on the Aleutian Islands, it was thought that the whole Pacific coast was in danger of invasion and all airports in British Columbia were put at military alert.[8]

As part of the joint defence plans, the United States, with its far greater resources, assumed responsibility for refurbishing facilities at several Canadian airports — with

8. The only time the west coast of Canada was in any danger was when a Japanese submarine impudently surfaced off Estavan Point, B.C., and shelled the lighthouse for thirty minutes. The air force at Victoria was alerted, but as the first bomber attempted to take-off it crashed on the runway, preventing the others from becoming airborne, and the submarine escaped.

American-built aircraft were collected at Canadian airports for ferrying to either the United Kingdom or the Soviet Union. Here at Dorval in Montreal are Venturas, B-24s, B-25s, and a B-17. (National Archives of Canada PA 114759)

its own agenda. The airports of Calgary, Edmonton, Whitehorse and Watson Lake benefited from this as thousands of USAF fighters and bombers went through them on their way to the Soviet Union. On the Atlantic coast, the large volume of traffic generated by American forces flying to the European theatre ensured that Gander, Goose Bay and Stephenville in Newfoundland were reconstructed and expanded. Lesser wartime projects such as the CANOL (Canadian Oil) pipeline and the Crimson Route (a more direct route over the Arctic to Europe) also caused airports to be built in otherwise inaccessible areas of Canada.

All told, the United States spent $100 million during the war on airport development in Canada. In 1945 Prime Minister Mackenzie King made sure that all U.S. facilities on Canadian soil were paid for and returned to federal control. The move cost his government $111 million, a vast sum then, some of it for airports that would have little value in peacetime. But as King said, it was a "down payment on Canadian sovereignty."

Historians may argue that without such crucial weapons as the jeep or the landing craft, victory over the Axis would have been more bloody and delayed. But without the airports in Canada to train thousands of BCATP aircrew, to ferry aircraft from the factory to the frontline, and to combat the U-boat menace, that victory might never have occurred. They were Canada's ultimate contribution to the war effort. With their superior resources, the British ran Bomber Command and the Americans dominated the Pacific theatre, but the BCATP and its airports were Canada's alone.

Airports in Peace

By the war's end, there were a total of 587 airports, airfields and air harbours in Canada. They ranged from three in Prince Edward Island to eighty in Ontario. As if to prove that the country was finally on a peacetime footing, in 1948, the Minister of Munitions C.D. Howe returned all aviation responsibilities to the Minister of Transport. Crown Assets Disposal quickly sold off those airports the military considered non-essential. At certain municipal airports, the runways, buildings and fuel dumps were handed over to the local community without charge. Some cities, like Toronto and Winnipeg, still could not afford to operate an airport and the Department of Transport continued as the landlord. Others, like Edmonton, Calgary and Regina, took control of their airports, but accepted federal subsidies to run them until the mid 1950s.

For certain airports, keeping the wartime momentum going was a priority. Cartierville, Malton, Winnipeg and Vancouver had built up large aircraft manufacturing industries during the war that had potential civilian use. Some idea of the expansion that took place at wartime airport plants might be seen at the Noorduyn factory at Cartierville, in the Montreal suburbs. In 1939, its workforce consisted of 110 men hand-building Norseman bushplanes. By V-J Day, Noorduyn's 11,000 workers had churned out 767 Norsemans and 2,800 Harvards on the same site. The Second World War transformed airports from farmers' fields to major economic generators that would have a social impact on the cities that had, in most cases, ignored their growth.

In 1944, in an effort to control the anticipated postwar boom in commercial aviation, the government set up the Air Transport Board. It would allocate routes and licence air carriers to operate from an airport. Thus empowered, the Board (and federal government) could make or break an airline . . . or an airport.

Once more, as after the First World War, surplus aircraft and unemployed aircrew caused flying clubs and small charter companies to flourish. Toronto Island Airport, for one, had its heyday, becoming for a short period the busiest airport in the country. But it was the arrival of passenger airliners such as the DC-4, the Lockheed Constellation and the Canadair North Star that forced the airports to shed their wartime image and adapt.

On 10 October, 1954, John Armistead Wilson, the Father of Canadian Airports died. He had emigrated from Scotland in 1911, the year of the great air meets. Through twenty-seven years of service, eventually becoming Direc-

Airliners like this Lockheed Constellation revolutionized air travel. Dorval's wartime terminal, in the background, was by 1954 becoming too small to cope with the number of passengers that such aircraft could carry. (Air Canada Archives)

tor of All Air Services in 1941, he guided government policy towards a national airport system. A professional engineer, through the 1920s Wilson travelled across most of Canada, by flying boat and railcar, surveying potential airfield sites and pressuring the politicians into building the Trans-Canada Airway. One of the members of the 1919 Air Board, he had seen airports evolve from grass strip and a windsock to the modern ribbons of concrete, futuristic control towers and noise-buffers.

The strategic bombing campaign during the war had created sophisticated runway lighting systems from approach lights to taxiways, and these soon became part of every large airport's equipment. In 1948 instrument landing systems (ILS) were introduced in Canada, transmitting beams along a glidepath making the pilot's decision to land easier. The ILS localiser, glide path indicators, and ground markers soon became familiar features at Toronto, Dorval, Winnipeg, Vancouver, Calgary and Lethbridge. By the mid-1960s sophisticated approach systems and runway lighting had been installed at sixteen airports, that could guide the aircraft to the ramp if it landed in very low visibility. Precision approach radar, aircraft hydrant refuelling that removed the need for gasoline bowsers, and airbridges between the aircraft and the terminal soon reshaped the airport complex beyond its postwar "make-do" dowdiness.

In 1946, the former RAF Ferry Command rooms at Dorval Airport terminal might have been sufficient for the few passengers that a Trans-Canada Airlines Lockheed 14 carried. A decade later when the Britannia and Viscount were introduced, vast changes in airport design were necessary. Where once ferry crews had dossed down, waiting for their bombers to be modified, the new breed of airport user demanded to be amused and cossetted between flights.

The steady rise in consumer income after the war had an enormous impact on air travel. As family incomes grew, larger proportions could be spent on vacations and air travel. Once the preserve of the wealthy, flying became democratised, and was put within reach of the middle class. The increasing number of vacationers drawn to using airliners required that not only longer runways or an ASDE radar be budgeted for by the airport accountant but attractive terminal buildings designed as well. ILS localisers and visual approach indicators were all very well for the aircrew but the amenities that the public could relate to were the new ticket counters, check-in facilities, transit lounges and shops. Like it or not, airports had to accommodate these new consumers.

The phenomenal popularity of air travel over sea and land (and thus airports over seaports and railway stations) can be measured by its impact on the more traditional forms

The rise in consumer income in the 1960s democratized flying, forcing airports to build new terminals. The new terminal at Dorval was ready in 1960. (Aeroports de Montréal Archives)

of transportation in North America. In 1967 as the DC-8s and Boeing 707s were bringing fairgoers to Dorval Airport to celebrate Canada's Centennial in Montreal, the Cunard liner *The Queen Mary* was on her last voyage across the Atlantic. The New York Central Railroad's *Twentieth Century Limited*, famed in song and movie, was being shunted off to the breaker's yard. In Canada, as the heavily subsidized, half-empty Canadian Pacific trains dwindled, the traveller turned to the airport. Between 1950 and 1990, the air share of the public transportation travel rose from fourteen per cent to ninety per cent. As late as 1955 aviation in Canada was still the domain of the wealthy or the military. Within a decade, it had metamorphosed into the latest form of mass transit, and the airports were forced to adapt.

Even without their commercial frills, the introduction of four-engined airliners to postwar airports had been devastating. The new aircraft's weight was important in determining the thickness and length of the runway, taxiway and apron. Runways had to be periodically rebuilt and extended, as the heavier the aircraft the longer the runway required. The pre-war DC-3 needed 4,500 feet (1,372 metres) to take-off but the Constellation of 1948 vintage required almost double that. The 1960s DC-8 lifted off at 10,000 feet (3,048 metres), while ten years later the Boeing 747-200B could only take-off on a runway of over 12,000 feet (3,658 metres). The competition demanded that flights across oceans and continents were now non-stop, and the heavy fuel loads that aircraft needed necessitated longer and longer take-off runs.

Although Canada had space to spare, the increasing runway lengths influenced the total land area that the airport required. It was poor timing. The inflating airports met the encroaching suburbs head on. Even as the housing developments were built to the boundaries of the original flying club/municipal airports, the arrival of jumbo jets dictated longer runways, wider car parks, more hangars and fleets of support vehicles.

Airports, that were already being criticised as voracious consumers of expensively flattened land, were now too large to be tucked away even in the outer suburbs of a city. Dorval Airport in Montreal and Blatchford Field in Edmonton were seen as too dangerous to the housing being built up around them. In their reincarnated forms airports were now exiled far out into the countryside, as Pickering was to have been for Toronto or Mirabel became for Montreal. Their subsequent rural locations meant the added expense of large car parks and/or being linked to their cities by mass transit systems.

With the piston-engine era, airliners like the Super Constellation carried nearly four times as many passengers as the pre-war DC-3. As post-war Malton coped with processing the seventy passengers off a Canadian Pacific DC-6, the Jet Age arrived with a Lufthansa Boeing 707 depositing 200 passengers at Passport Control. Suddenly there were lineups at Customs and luggage pile-ups at the baggage carousels. Security checks, health and immigration control points all disrupted the smooth flow of passengers in and out of the terminal. The problem didn't end when the passengers were funnelled out of the restricted zones. Public areas also had to be large enough to accommodate the meeters and the greeters, the passengers' friends and families, estimated by cautious authorities to be quadruple those travelling. By 1975, Canadian airport planners had to meet the reality of an Air India Boeing 747 disgorging 600 passengers into its corridors at peak travel time, even as they accommodated a Bearskin Airways C-46 depositing as few as fifteen.

While the Department of Transport sought frantically to adapt existing airport facilities to wide-body jets measuring 196 feet (60 metres) from wing-tip to wing-tip, an airport building boom was set in motion. To complement their endless runways, the airports of the 1960s acquired whole new vocabularies. Jetways, hub-and-spoke, fingers, satellites — all became part of what two decades earlier was a hangar and a farmhouse.

Airports had to adapt to the next generation of aircraft, and quickly. The 1960s was the first full decade of commercial jet travel, and it changed airport design and management radically. Even the wingspan and fuselage length of the Boeing 747, DC-10 and Concorde affected the size of the parking aprons required, which in turn influenced the configuration and design of the terminal building. Toronto International Airport authorities realized too late that as aesthetically pleasing as their aeroquay was, it could not accommodate the many jumbo-jets that soon crowded around it.

Sadly, none of the architects that designed the new terminal buildings in this country showed any of the imagination of the Finnish-American architect Eero Saarineen. As early as 1956, with his TWA winged building at JFK Airport, Saarinen showed it was possible to break away from the rectilinear concrete and glass shells that all other airport terminals were. It may be argued that Toronto's Aeroquay and later Atrium were the only buildings to compromise function with flair.

Gradually, speciality shops, car rental agencies and interfaith chapels ousted the traditional hard-bench waiting room and greasy spoon café from the terminal. Where once all activity at the site had centred around a lone figure in goggles and leather-jacket who heaved mail sacks into a wood and wire Puss Moth, now magazine racks and video arcades demanded the public's attention.

It was a case of airports having to grow to suit the aircraft manufacturers' designs. The development of moving sidewalks and mobile lounges helped buy the airport designers some time as they redrew their architectural plans. Cries of "Why can't Boeing design for the airport instead of the other way around?" were heard through the 1970s. "Would General Motors or Ford," airport managers asked, "build a bus too big for the city streets it was supposed to travel on?"

Once airports had grown haphazardly, but now they were given birth by master plans that took into account not only the width and weight of the aircraft but also the concerns of the region that airport lay in. There were noise restrictions over the encroaching suburbs, fear of bird-strikes and an awareness of the environment: glycol used to de-ice the aircraft could not be drained into the local sewers.

The airport has brought about sociological changes to Canada almost as important as the port and railroad station. Only the private automobile has affected the national fabric more. Such "airport cities" as Pearson, Dorval and Vancouver employ thousands of people and have their own banks, radio stations and police forces. Pearson International alone accounts for 56,000 jobs, $1.9 billion in income and $630 million in tax revenue. Once viewed as drains on the metropolitan area they served (even before privatization) the airport–city relationship had been radically altered. They had been reborn as cash cows for politicans at all levels.

In 1938, with the arrival of the DC-3, Toronto newspaper editors complained that local airports were not keeping up with passenger growth, that a quart of air travel was being squeezed into a pint pot. American editors were even more melodramatic about poor airport facilities below the border: "We are putting eagles in wren's nests!" one wrote. With airports straining at the seams today, the rhetoric, and the problem, remains depressingly the same. Air travel is estimated to grow in North America alone at seven per cent annually, and imaginative solutions will have to be implemented — quickly.

In 1996, the air traveller at Pearson, Mirabel, Vancouver and Dorval can be sure of congestion in the terminal concourse and the frustration of finding his luggage, let alone his car in the enormous car park outside. But when compared to the miracle he is witness to, the picking up of millions of people in one city and flying them to another, it seems a small price to pay.

Winging it with Privatization, CAATS and Open Skies

Now in the last years of the century that created it, the airport is approaching its own mid-life crisis. Billions of dollars will soon have to be pumped into its sagging infrastructure, to upgrade communications, mass transit and environmental safeguards. To the Canadian public still caught in a recession, airports and their users appear wealthy and privileged. Why should they get special treatment and suck up tax dollars better spent on hospitals and kindergartens? Their very size and complexities have made them difficult to comprehend. Now even Ottawa had lost the political will to operate them.

It would take until the late 1980s for the federal government to acknowledge what the taxpayer had guessed all along: that much of the national air transportation system was oversubsidized and under-used. Of the 726 certified airports in Canada, only twenty-six were used by ninety-four per cent of the travelling public — the other 700 catering to a mere six per cent. It was a waste of financial resources that recession-battered economies worldwide could no longer afford. As the rail and maritime transportation systems had been, Canadian airports are heavily subsidized: in this case at a cost of $2.3 billion annually. By a series of pre- and post-war policies, ad hoc decisions and plain political pork-barrelling, by 1989 the federal government owned, operated or financially contributed to 150 of those 726 airports.

To its credit, the Department of Transport had worked on a comprehensive plan in the 1970s to commercialize Canadian airports. The final decision to implement the scheme was to be made by the Liberal government of Pierre Trudeau, at the Cabinet level. There it was dismissed out of hand, by ministers who rationalized that in some of their ridings the airport was sometimes the only federal presence and employer.

Twenty years later, faced with a massive national deficit and an economy in transition, the federal government developed two initiatives to deal with replacing the present air transportation system for an integrated, more affordable one. The first dealt with changing the national air navigation system and the second was the National Airports Policy (NAP). Under it, Ottawa would no longer be the owner and operator of airports but an owner and landlord. The twenty-six major airports, known as the National Airport System (NAS), would still belong to the federal government, but now they would be leased to local authorities for a period of sixty years. The twenty-six were those in the provincial capitals and such busy airports as Dorval, Mirabel and Thunder Bay.

The basic concept was that if they were locally operated, airports would be more responsive to regional needs and forced to function cost-effectively. Metropolitan authorities like the Greater Toronto Airport Authority would inherit Department of Transport-built large airports, while smaller regional airports (that have scheduled passenger traffic but handle less than 200,000 passengers annually) would be offered for sale to local municipal governments, commissions or businesses. Beginning in 1995, over a five year period, these airports would gradually lose their federal subsidies. Typical of the smaller airports are Hamilton and Toronto Island, Ontario and Goose Bay, Labrador.

Only the airports in remote areas of the country that serve as lifelines for the local community would continue to receive federal assistance. Kuujjuaq (Fort Chimo) Quebec, Sandspit BC, Yellowknife NWT, and Whitehorse Yukon were some of those designated. These would be helped out by a capital assistance grant of between $30–35 million, which would come from the revenues generated by the twenty-six big airports.

In its simplest form, the privatization of an airport is when management or ownership is transferred from the public sector to the private one.[9] The federal government is thus relieved of the financial burden of supporting it, and the market competition generated will stimulate the local economy. Airport resources would be more efficiently utilized and used to increase the revenues produced by commercial enterprises on site. Furthermore, because of the private sector profit motivation, there would be cost savings in airport management, both in the air and land sides.

In 1992, four airport groups were privatized and now operate Vancouver, Calgary, Edmonton and the two airports at Montreal (Dorval and Mirabel). A second wave of privatisation began three years later and, if all went according to plan, the federal government was scheduled to transfer control of Toronto's Pearson, Ottawa's Macdonald-Cartier and Winnipeg International to their respective airport authorities by 1 April 1996.

The sixty-year lease is meant to provide the authorities with enough incentive (and revenue) to modernize the passenger terminals and runways. In anticipation of their independance, several airports have gone on spending binges. Vancouver Airport, in its self-appointed mission to become the Asia-Pacific gateway to North America, has already spent $102 million to build a parallel runway to increase its annual operations from 275,000 to 425,000 movements. The runway and other capital improvements are being financed by a special tax on passengers who use the airport. The tax ranges from $5 for passengers from within the province to $15 for overseas. There is the added inconvenience of having to pay at special booths after purchasing the airline ticket. Despite this, international air traffic into Vancouver is booming: the Open Skies Agreement will result in the addition of twenty-three daily transborder flights and 400,000 extra passengers that will translate into more than $5 million revenue annually.[10]

Other privatized (or soon to be) airports have also began casting around for ways of raising cash for improvements with mixed results. Typical is the Edmonton International authority's scheme. The new terminal that it wants by 1998 will cost $150 million, and a tax of $2 per passenger would go a long way to paying for it. Unfortunately, the city's municipal airport (Blatchford) is still outside the authority's control. Airlines and passengers would be quick to divert to it if such a tax were to be imposed.

At Calgary International Airport the management has a wish list ranging from expanding the runway apron and

9. The private sector does not even have to be local. When the Australian government recently put its twenty-seven biggest airports on sale, the sale attracted several foreign buyers, of which BAA (the British Aircraft Authority) was the strongest contender.

10. Jim Bagnell, *Flight International* 26 April 1995 p.37-38

refurbishing the holding rooms, to adding three extra gates and improving the car parks. This ten-year, $110 million capital spending program would, like Vancouver, also be funded by a passenger surcharge. The airlines that use Calgary are fighting this as they fear customers would blame them for the extra tax.

The best showcases of the early benefits of privatization are Montreal's Dorval and Mirabel airports. In 1994 their authority, Aeroports de Montréal, achieved a $26 million surplus on a revenue of $100 million. Given that most of the surplus was not generated by Vancouver-type surcharges, this is all the more remarkable. Even more amazing, almost half of the surplus came from the under-used, much abused Mirabel Airport. The explanation would gladden the heart of privatization lobbyists everywhere: Mirabel's traffic was mainly international, so passengers tended to check in for their flights earlier and thus spent more time and money at the airport shops, bars and restaurants. But even at the two airports, the "leaner meaner" environment is apparent: when the authority took them over from the government, it cut the staff from 560 employees to 510.

The older Dorval Airport has benefitted from this financial surplus. A refurbished passenger lobby for the anticipated increase in trans-border traffic, a marque for rain protection, and the installation of electronic kiosks to expedite parking payments are some of the projects that were paid for and completed. With profits being ploughed into capital improvements, it is what Ottawa envisions privatization to be.

But no matter who owns or operates the airports, there was little that could be done about increasing air traffic congestion. High above the country, far out in the oceans, hundreds of aircraft are plying crowded flight paths, aiming for specific airports. Hundreds more are maneuvering out of their parking bays at those airports, attempting to keep on schedule and take-off into their designated flight path.

For the frustrated passengers buckled up in an idling Air Canada DC-9, waiting to taxi out, all this is unimportant. They cannot see the busy flight paths or airways above filled with military aircraft, subsonic airliners and propeller-driven recreation aircraft weaving around one another. These are corridors within which aircraft are protected by internationally agreed rules of separation. Other aircraft must be at least 1,000 feet (305 metres) above or below, ten minutes flying time in front and behind, and ten minutes on either side. In a daily juggling act, the 2,200 Canadian air traffic controllers manually process weather information, satellite images, radar, voice transmissions and flight plans. As the number of aircraft have multiplied, the controllers increased the spacing between their charges on the airways, thus causing massive congestion on the ground.

Air traffic control is an integral part of every major airport and was operated by the federal government twenty-four hours a day and 365 days a year. Until it began to privatize the industry in 1995, Transport Canada ran it entirely and is even today ultimately responsibile for its efficiency and safety. But at a time when new technolgies were offering great advances in safety, Canadian air traffic controllers were continuing to rely on thirty year old equipment.

In 1989, with air traffic within Canada growing at a rate of seventeen per cent annually, Ottawa launched the ambitious $660 million Canadian Automated Air Traffic System (CAATS). When completed, it would be able to track thousands of aircraft electronically and assign flight positions and take-off slots. In this way, it would cut the distance between aircraft by more than half, saving the passengers time and airlines money. All the data that controllers now process manually would be fed into data-processing systems at seven control centres. This would be accessed at the sixty busiest airports across the country by controllers from their individual workstations. The heart of the system was to be a sophisticated artificial intelligence, that included a crucial "conflict resolution" feature to

The deceptive calm of an airport control tower belies the daily juggling act in the skies above. Canada's 2,200 air traffic controllers process streams of aircraft through increasingly crowded skies. (Ottawa Airport Authority photo)

prevent aircraft from colliding. Transport Canada estimated that once in place CAATS would save the government, and the airlines, at least $1.5 billion.

The government currently loses $200 million annually running the network of control towers and radar stations. A potential source of revenue was to charge foreign airlines for overflying Canada. Over 800 flights arc over Canadian airspace daily as they fly in or out of North America. All are tracked by Canadian air traffic controllers and as of

1 November 1994, each airline was charged between $2 and $5 for each passenger they carried over Canadian airspace. It was an attempt to help defray the spiralling cost of air traffic control — and CAATS.

In December 1989, the contract for CAATS was awarded to Hughes Aircraft Ltd. for a fixed price of $377 million. Founded by American aviation pioneer Howard Hughes in 1932, Hughes Aircraft was a defence contractor without any experience in air traffic control. But the company did promise to employ thousands of Canadians in recession-hit western Canada. Ministers from that region in Prime Minister Brian Mulroney's government, who had seen their ridings miss out on the major government contracts of the 1980s — like CF-18 repairs and frigate construction — now felt it was their turn to dip into Ottawa's largesse.

What subsequently developed was reminiscent of the Avro Arrow scandal. By 1995, CAATS was still no more than a pile of blueprints, and air traffic congestion at major Canadian airports had become as notorious as New York's Kennedy Airport. The federal government was becoming so concerned about delays and soaring costs, that it stopped payments to Hughes. The American company defended itself, by claiming it could not keep up with the changes in specifications that Transport Canada continually wanted and that since 1990 it had ordered up to 5,300 changes.

Hughes wanted Ottawa to first pay for these changes before it delivered anything at all. It also wanted Transport Canada to assume installation and training costs at the sixty chosen airports.

Impatient and embittered, the prospective new owners of the privatized airports had also lost heart with CAATS. They wanted the whole project to be scrapped and re-thought, this time with their input. Finally, the Canadian taxpayers, who had watched as Ottawa spent $400 million on a pile of blueprints, were left wondering what went wrong, and how much more they would have to pay for a safe, efficient air traffic control system.

Canadian airports came of age and entered the cruel world of deficit reduction and self-financing in the mid-1990s when the federal government stopped subsidizing them. Control tower operations were commercialized and the foreign airlines they tracked were now billed for the right to fly over Canadian air space. With the national air traffic control system losing $200 million annually, Transport Canada was quick to unload it onto a non-profit corporation called Nav Canada for $1.5 billion.

To further trim the deficit, Transport Canada closed down its firefighting stations at smaller airports like Churchill, Manitoba and Yarmouth, Nova Scotia, and scaled down emergency response units at regional airports like

Charlottetown, PEI and Victoria, BC. As they had done half a century before, these airports would now have to rely on their municipal fire departments to handle aviation fires. While critics point out that in some cases, the nearest suburban fire station is now more than thirty minutes away, the move is in keeping with the government's logic that if the community wanted an airport it had to support it. Fortunately, the major international airports like Pearson, Dorval and Calgary, through which ninety-four per cent of air travellers transit, are subject to International Civil Aviation Organisation (ICAO) standards and are not affected.

Airports in Canada are undergoing a metamorphis as the expected air traffic flood caused by Open Skies materializes. After twenty years of negotiations, the Open Skies agreement was signed by US President Bill Clinton and Prime Minister Jean Chrétien on 24 February 1995. Disarming in its simplicity, the treaty gives US and Canadian airlines unlimited route-rights to any of each other's cities. Canadian airlines would have complete access to all US cities and US airlines have access to all Canadian cities — including, in a few years, the rich markets of Toronto, Montreal and Vancouver.

Bureaucrats on both sides of the border were lavish in self-congratulation. Transport Minister Doug Young attributed the success of the Agreement to his giving the negotiators "a free hand" in the haggling. Aviation analysts know better. The real reason that Open Skies became a reality is that it was a logical progression of recent airline deregulation: the dismantling of the monopolistic and protective laws that kept air service between Canada and the United States low and prices high. Airlines like Air Canada that had profited by decades of monopolising air routes, and creating their own artificially high fares, suddenly found themselves near bankruptcy.

Regional markets now looked especially attractive to the airlines: offering unlimited possibilities for the smaller airports on both sides of the border. For example, before Open Skies, a trip from Winnipeg to Cheyenne, Wyoming meant a flight first to Minneapolis, then another airline to Denver and finally a third carrier to Cheyenne. Now, if the market warranted, city to city non-stop flights are possible. More choices and cheaper airfares will bring both nations closer to each other. The effect on Canadian airports of the anticipated millions of travellers brought by Open Skies in the near future remains to be seen.

Whatever the role of the airport may be, the country can only gain. In May, 1995 the Canadian Urban Institute held a conference to review the status of the Toronto Island Airport. The findings held that if the airport were upgraded, and allowed to compete properly, it would generate $210 million a year in new taxes for governments at all levels, 29,000 new jobs and $500 million in new employment income and would add $1 billion annually to the province's gross domestic product. In short it would become a much needed local economic generator, as has Pearson International.

Today, the nation desperately needs an economic boost to turn the economy around. Airports if properly managed, underwrite the prosperity of their surrounding regions — often to their own detriment. As institutions their contributions to the well-being of this country, during war and peace, have been documented, but rarely recognized.

Calgary

As with other cities, Calgary went through a succession of airports and airport terminals, each more expansive (and expensive) than its predecessor. Flying in Calgary began in the summer of 1914 with two young men, Frank Ellis[1] and Tom Blakeley, who spent all their free time at Bowness Park, ten kilometres (6 miles) west of Calgary. There they set about repairing a wrecked Curtiss pusher aircraft. They christened it *The West Wind* and took to the air in it on 25 July, 1915. The following summer Ellis and Blakeley moved to Shouldice Park, also in the west of the city, and began to refine their aircraft's controlling techniques. Several crashes later the Curtiss finally fell apart and Ellis[1] and Blakeley left Calgary to seek their fortunes elsewhere.

Bowness Park was also used as a landing field by Captain Ernest Hoy during the first trans-Canada flight in August, 1919. By 1922, the Park was an airfield about eighty-four metres square and its tenants were Fred McCall and Jack Palmer, two World War I pilots who earned their living as barnstormers. In September 1928, McCall flew in the city's first air show for the Calgary Aero Club, using their field on the Banff Coach Road. The airfield was much too windy for flying, and when the city opened another at Renfrew in 1929 the club moved there. Renfrew was the first of Calgary's airports to have a hangar, still discernible at the corner of 12th Avenue and 6th Street NE. Two air companies, Great Western Airways and Rutledge Airways operated out of Renfrew and, because the airport was used for airmail routes, the federal government built all-weather runways and a radio range.

In 1938, Calgary's fourth airport was chosen. Six hundred acres (240 hectares) were purchased by the city council northeast of the city and named McCall Field. Trans-Canada Airlines (TCA) had just been created and the council hoped that it could be routed through Calgary, rather than Lethbridge. But TCA decided to use Leth-

---

1. Frank Ellis became Canada's foremost aviation historian. His book *Canada's Flying Heritage*, remains the basis for any study on early aviation in this country.

Originally named after Fred McCall, a local barnstormer, Calgary Airport welcomed the first Trans-Canada Airlines DC-8 in 1962. (Air Canada Archives)

bridge, because the Rockies immediately west of it were not as steep as those near Calgary. A feeder line to Calgary was thought sufficient and services to Lethbridge and later Edmonton were begun. The city built a hangar which doubled as a passenger terminal and maintenance area.

When World War II began, the Department of Transport took over Calgary airport, although unlike Edmonton it always remained a civil operation. The RAF, the RCAF and the United States Air Force all used Calgary as a staging route to Alaska, or as part of the British Commonwealth Air Training Plan (BCATP), and hangars and ramps were built to accommodate them. When the USAF and RAF moved out in 1945, they left behind five large hangars and various buildings.

In 1948, with more powerful DC-3s, TCA was able to negotiate the Rockies at Calgary and shifted its base to the airport. The timing was unfortunate: the Fraser River flooded its valley and all available aircraft were requisitioned to fly sandbags to the hardest-hit areas to stem the waters in Operation Sandbag. The resulting heavy traffic destroyed the main runway at Calgary Airport and, once more, TCA shifted back to Lethbridge.

During the war, the USAF had built a broad concrete ramp on the west side of the airport as an assembly point for its aircraft being ferried to Alaska. In 1949, the abandoned U.S. buildings on the ramp's perimeter were adapted for use as a passenger terminal: Calgary Airport's first. But they soon proved inadequate for the traffic. In 1950, Canadian Pacific Airlines connected Calgary with the interior of British Columbia and, to cope with the influx of passengers, a new terminal was opened in 1956.

The airport's name was changed by the City Council to Calgary International Airport, McCall Field in 1962. It had become truly international with Hughes Air West flying in from Seattle, and Canadian Pacific Airlines beginning its Calgary-Amsterdam services. With heavier runways and technical improvements necessary, the City Council could no longer afford to pay for updating airport facilities and in 1967 Transport Canada took the airport over. The government extended the old facilities and then built a completely new terminal building in 1977.

In 1969, as Calgary coped with the arrival of jets, all small aircraft were moved to a satellite airport built at Springbank, eight miles (13 kilometres) west of the city. By the time Calgary hosted the Olympic Games in 1988, a new air traffic control tower had been built, an international finger had been added and KLM, Lufthansa (briefly), Delta and United Airlines were all using the airport.

Edmonton

Edmonton was involved with flying as early as 29 April 1911, when Hugh Robinson took off from the Edmonton Exhibition Grounds in an aircraft resembling a Wright Flyer. In 1916, American aviator Katherine Stinson gave aerobatic performances on the same grounds. She is better remembered for having made history by landing at the Exhibition Grounds from Calgary on 9 July 1918 with the first airmail.

After the First World War, pilots and aircraft were plentiful and aviation companies sprang up across Canada. In Edmonton, "Wop" May,[1] the famous bush pilot, leased a few acres of farmland on the old St. Albert Trail in the northwestern area of the city for his May Airplanes Ltd. The Edmonton Airplane Co. also set up at Hagmann's Farm at the corner of Portage Avenue. Both airfields remained in use through the 1920s.

In 1920, the United States Army Air Service chose May's airfield, over Hagmann's Farm, for its flights to Alaska. The first four American aircraft to fly from New York to Nome, Alaska and back were scheduled to land at Edmonton on 27 July 1920. In this age of celebrity flights, throngs of citizens came to the airport and an official reception was made ready to receive them. Wop May even took the mayor of Edmonton up in his JN-4 to escort them in. However, to the four American airmen, one field looked as good as another, and they headed for a farmer's field, northeast of the city. May followed them down, with the mayor frantically signalling the Americans not to land there. This probably confused the visitors even more and they made for the nearest field below them. May landed with them and explained they were expected at his airfield. After a laugh, all five aircraft took off and landed a few minutes later at the "official airfield" before the crowds.

Later that year, May went to New York to fly back two Junkers bought by Imperial Oil Ltd., hoping the aircraft

---

1.Wilfrid Reid (Wop) May had flown with 209 Squadron on the Western Front and narrowly escaped becoming the last victim of Manfred von Richthofen, the dreaded Red Baron.

Edmonton's Blatchford Airport has been the scene of many historic events in Canadian aviation. This terminal building dates from 1943 and was demolished in 1975, a year before the fiftieth anniversary of the airport. (Air Canada Archives)

would be based at his field as well. In 1921, his luck ran out and Imperial Oil took over the airfield at Hagmann's Farm. In 1924, Mayor Kenny Blatchford won the approval of the Air Board to make this site Edmonton's municipal airport. Called Blatchford Field, it was inaugurated in style on a wintry day in January 1927 when two RCAF Siskin fighters from High River, one piloted by Punch Dickins, landed on the snow-covered runway.

That year the Edmonton & Northern Alberta Aero Club was formed to run the airport. The Club hired Wop May as an instructor and graduated more pilots than any other club in Canada. The City of Edmonton spent $35,000 on runways, a pair of substantial hangars and, to prepare for the airmail contract, runway lighting. Hangar No. 1 was built with its distinctive three storey tower, and would not have been out of place at a European airport. Well sited on the supply route for the Mackenzie and Peace River areas, Blatchford was fast becoming the busiest airport in Canada.

On 3 January 1929, Blatchford Field was the scene of a dramatic rescue flight to save a distant town from a fatal epidemic. To prevent diptheria from spreading through the region, antitoxin had to be flown immediately to Fort Vermillion, from where it could be taken by dogsled to the Little Red River settlement. Although it was minus forty degrees Fahrenheit (minus forty Celsius) and a blizzard was due, the Department of Health asked May and his partner, Vic Horner, to transport the antitoxin. The pair had just received their new Avro Avian from the manufacturer in England and it still had an open cockpit!

They took off from Blatchford Airport, heavily overburdened with the protected medicine. The 600-mile (950-kilometre) flight was made through blizzard conditions, with the faces of both men scarred and bleeding from being whipped by the wind in the open cockpits. But the little Avian landed at the Fort as darkness set in and the antitoxin was rushed by dogteam to the settlement. May and Horner returned to Edmonton the next day, to find they had become heroes across Canada. There were more than 5,000 people waiting to greet them at the airport.

In 1930, the city took Blatchford over from the club and hired Jimmy Bell as its first manager. Bell is especially remembered for his part in the events of 30 June, 1931. The day before, American aviators Wiley Post and Harold Gatty had landed at Blatchford Field to refuel on their round-the-world flight. Because of overnight rain, the runway had become too soft, and Post and Gatty could not take-off from it and still keep their schedule. Bell had the overhead wires removed from the poles along the adjacent paved Portage Avenue so the pilots could use the street as a runway. Post's account of his takeoff from Edmonton makes for stirring reading:

"As we warmed up the engine, the rain stopped. The ship was towed out to the sidewalk and a pair of Mounties dashed up and down the street in an automobile, clearing away all the traffic. I taxied out onto the unused street car tracks and faced the nose towards the hotel two miles away, at which we had stayed . . . I let the Wasp have her head. Curbstones and electric light poles clipped by the wingtips so fast that I was a little scared myself . . . Within 15 seconds the outlying houses had dropped away. By the time we had reached the first turn in the street, we had a good 500 feet and as I came over the Hotel MacDonald, where our late maitre d'hotel was on the roof with his whole army of bellhops in array to salute us going by, the ground dropped away fast, and we turned over the high bluff which the hotel tops."[1]

---

1. Christopher Chant. *Aviation An Illustrated History*. London. Orbis Publishing 1983. page 159

No history of Edmonton Airport could be complete without mentioning George William (Grant) McConachie. McConachie's exploits capture the bushflying era that centered around Edmonton between the wars. As a boy, McConachie had hung around Blatchford airfield, doing odd jobs for Punch Dickins and Wop May, and ultimately learning to fly with the Edmonton and Northern Alberta Aero Club in 1929. McConachie formed his own air company, Independant Airways, to haul fish from the northern Saskatchewan lakes to Edmonton. It was an unenviable job, with the aircraft's fuselage stinking, and if it were not immediately hosed down the fabric would rot away!

On 30 November 1932, as he was taking off from Blatchford Airport, McConachie's Fokker Universal stalled and crashed on its nose. He was hospitalised, the aircraft written off and the fish hauling contract cancelled. Later, when the company's other aircraft was seized by the sheriff for bad debts, Independant Airways closed down. Undaunted, McConachie began another air company, United Air Transport, and in 1937 linked Edmonton in a scheduled run with Whitehorse, NWT. Ten years later, McConachie would become President of Canadian Pacific Airlines with his boyhood hero, Punch Dickins, as General Manager.

During the Second World War, Edmonton was taken over by the Department of Transport and used as a base for aircrew training under the British Commonwealth Air Training Plan. The many Ansons and Fleet Finches being used, and crashed, forced the DND to open an aircraft repair depot on the northside of the airport, the site becoming the nucleus for aero manufacturers for decades after.

The City of Edmonton had, from the days of Mayor K.A. Blatchford, always been aviation-minded and supportive of its airport. In 1941, while Montreal and Toronto were relying on federal largesse to expand their airports, Edmonton raised $92,000 to build an impressive two storey terminal at the airport. The building had a control tower, offices for both Trans-Canada and Canadian Pacific Airlines and it housed the airport administration.

More than anything else, it was the arrival of the United States Air Force that really changed the airport. Edmonton was a major refuelling base on the Northwest Staging Route the USAF used to ferry aircraft to Alaska and then to the Soviet Union. The USAF built its own hangars on the east side, but so many of its aircraft were flying through (sometimes 800 a day) that it eventually built its own air base at Namao, north of the city and moved out of Blatchford in 1945. After the war all the RCAF's military activities were also transferred from Blatchford to Namao.

With the war's end, the City of Edmonton took control of its airport once more, with the Department of Transport providing a small financial subsidy. By 1957, even this aid was unnecessary as Blatchford was busy enough to become entirely self-supporting.

With the dawning of the jet age and the passenger boom, both the City of Edmonton and the Department of Transport began to look at closing down Blatchford and relocating further from the city. The suburbs had crept up around the old airport and there was legitimate concern as to danger from air traffic in a built-up area. Then too, the wide expanse of land the airport stood on was now worth a fortune on the property market. However, when several of the airport's tenants refused to move and the American consultants hired by the city recommended that Blatchford be kept open as an "industrial" field, the airport was saved.

In 1963, Blatchford became Edmonton Industrial Airport with Pacific Western Airlines as the only scheduled carrier. International aviation was moved to the new Edmonton International Airport and recreational and flying training to Villeneuve Airport, northwest of the city. Sadly in 1975, a year before the airport's fiftieth anniversary, the old wartime terminal was demolished. Torn down too were the old hangars built in 1929. While no architectural beauties, they represented an era in the airport's history that had

A "Canadian" Boeing 737 at the terminal. Grant McConachie, the founder of Canadian Pacific Airlines began flying at Edmonton's Blatchford Field in 1932. (Roth and Ramberg Photography)

Edmonton International Airport

To relieve the congestion of Blatchford Field, in 1955 the Department of Transport and the City of Edmonton decided to construct a new airport fifteen miles (24 kilometres) south of Edmonton. Two runways, 11-29 and 01-19, were completed by 1960 and the airport was opened on 15 February, 1964 by the Minister of Transport, J.W. Pickersgill. Perhaps demonstrating who had put up the most money, the first aircraft to land at the new airport was the Department of Transport's DC-3.

Built in the obligatory 1960s stainless steel and glass mode, the terminal had a feature unique to the oil-producing region of Alberta. On the passenger side, sculptor Norman Slater created a rotating steel shaft, sixty feet (18 metres) high with actual gas flames shooting out of it.

Under-utilized when it opened for the North Stars and Constellations of the day, the terminal came into its own with the jet age. The DC-8s and Boeing 707s of Air Canada, Canadian Pacific and later Wardair brought the thousands of customers that soon made the new terminal pay for itself. In the early 1970s, Alberta was experiencing an oil boom and this was reflected at the airport. Imperial and Panarctic Oil companies both built their own freight and

also vanished — bush pilots and barnstormers, Wiley Post and Wop May. The Edmonton Historical Board however recognised the airport's past by designating Blatchford Field a historical site.

Today, Edmonton Municipal Airport is in the heart of the city it serves. It has an efficient re-clearance facility to enable passengers to clear US Customs and Immigration. Like Hamilton Airport, Ontario and Dorval, Quebec, it has found its own niche: serving the regional market.

Alberta's oil boom in the 1970s was reflected in the fortunes of Edmonton Airport. Companies like Imperial, Panarctic, and Wardair all expanded their facilities. (Roth & Ramberg Photo)

passenger terminals in 1972 to support their aviation operations in the north.

In 1976, Wardair put up its own hangar for servicing its 747 fleet and Marathon Air Terminals completed an airfreight terminal to cope with the increasing load of cargo. After Toronto, Dorval and Vancouver, Edmonton became the fourth busiest passenger airport in Canada. In 1980, over 2.5 million passengers were using the terminal building, causing a $21 million expansion.

Strategically situated to be the northern gateway for the North American Free Trade Agreement and on the Great Circle Route to Europe, Edmonton International developed its cargo facilities making them the second largest in Canada. Air freight companies liked the twenty-four-hour operations and access to a trans-border truck interface system. In 1993, 23,620 tons (24,000 tonnes) were processed through its two dozen cargo-related companies. ICC Edmonton, the International Commercial Centre launched an aggressive campaign to become a duty-free trade zone.

With parents like Wop May, Jimmy Bell and Kenny Blatchford, Edmonton's two airports cannot but succeed in the brave new world of the National Airports Policy and Open Skies.

Gander

In 1935, the governments of Canada, the United Kingdom, and Ireland committed themselves to the creation of a landplane air service over the Atlantic Ocean within three years. Although Alcock and Brown had conquered it in a Vickers Vimy bomber on 14 June, 1919, sixteen years later a scheduled passenger service across the Atlantic was still only in the planning stages — and that with flying boats. American and British airlines planned to operate flying boats from Foynes, Ireland to Botwood, Newfoundland, and from there either to New York or Montreal. In 1936 Botwood was equipped with powerful radio facilities to guide in the flying boats.

As luxurious and romantic as they were, the flying boats were limited operationally to flights during the summer months. Far-sighted aviation officials on both sides of the Atlantic understood that the gracious "Clippers" were only a stopgap measure until landplanes with sufficient range could be designed. In any case, there were still no airports in either Ireland or Newfoundland that these landplanes

could use. The British, however, confidently expected by 1937 to have their De Havilland Albatross landplane ready to be put in service on the trans-Atlantic route. It was to have a sufficiently long range and passenger capacity to make a scheduled Atlantic flight economically feasible. Accordingly, as Newfoundland was part of the British Empire, the Air Ministry in London sent a survey party to the island to scout out a site for a suitable airfield.

On 11 August 1935, a De Havilland Gypsy Moth droned over the interior of the island. It carried two British Air Ministry officials and was piloted by Captain Douglas Fraser, a Newfoundlander who was familiar with the terrain. Fraser had already done aerial surveys of Botwood for the British government and later would survey Argentia for the United States Navy. For these and other aerial feats, in 1987 he would be inducted into Canada's Aviation Hall of Fame.

The party selected a site near Gander Lake that Fraser knew had good weather conditions. While there were no roads to it, the Newfoundland railway line passed through and the site was marked on the map as Milepost 213. A thick forest covered the uneven ground and the Air Ministry's accountant submitted an estimate for the clearing of the trees and levelling of the site. The cost was approved by the Director General of the Air Ministry, Sir Francis Shlemerdine, a former Indian Army cavalry officer who, it is thought, knew little about airfields and less of Newfoundland. Unfortunately, it was later discovered the estimate did not include digging out the roots of the trees, which effectively doubled the price. It is reputed the scouting party's financial manager took the only honourable course open to him: he committed suicide.

At about the same time, the British government learnt the De Havilland Albatross was unsuitable to fly the Atlantic. Nevertheless, the funds had been allocated and such was the faith of both governments in the progress of aviation that planning of the airport's construction went ahead. The airport was to be built by the government of Newfoundland, with the British government paying five-sixths of the capital costs and half of the annual operating expenses. Imperial Airways (the British government) also transferred their radio station and staff from Botwood to the new airport.

Then a third party entered into the birth of Gander Airport. After the costly failure of the airship base at St. Hubert outside Montreal, the Canadian government was reluctant to finance any more airports. But it realized Newfoundland was of strategic importance to Maritime Canada, and as a result it limited its contribution to the Atlantic air route to providing some meteorological forecasting for Gander.

Work crews began arriving at Mile Post 213 in the summer of 1936. The fifty construction workers and engineers initially lived in the railcars that brought them to the site, before putting up rude cabins for the winter. Faced with such a huge undertaking, the Newfoundland government hired engineers with experience on another giant project, the Welland Canal.

Work on the airport came to a halt during the harsh winter of 1936-37, but with spring the heavy equipment arrived and the construction crew increased to 500. A railway station was built at the site and soon a small city of tents sprang up for the construction crews. Because there were no roads to Gander, the railway remained the airport personnel's only link with the outside world. The airport was not yet called Gander, but officially known as Newfoundland Airport, Newfoundland. To the locals however, the site chosen would always be Hattie's Corner, after a woodcutter who lived nearby, and sometimes Cobb's Camp for a family that lived two miles (3 kilometres) away.

The failure of the Albatross did not deter the planners and the work continued through 1937 as the airport began to take shape. It was built on a grand scale with four paved runways, making it the largest paved airport in the world. The main runway was 4,800 by 1,200 feet (1,463 by 366 metres) in length, and the others 4,500 by 600 feet (1,372 by 183 metres). As this was the only paved runway in Newfoundland, and it was expected that after the completion of a trans-Atlantic flight an aircraft would have little fuel to find an alternate airport, an advanced Lorenz blind landing system was installed. A forerunner to the instrument landing system (ILS), the Lorenz was a German invention and made by Telefunken. Given that both countries were then sliding into war, it is surprising the patent had been sold to Marconi of England.

At the centre of Gander airport, a three storey building with a rudimentary control tower was built. Looking more like a school building, it contained the offices for the administration of the airport and rooms for single staff. It also became the focus of all community life at the airport: serving as a bar, movie theatre and dance hall. Married staff lived in houses along the airport perimeter and a general store, a fire station and post office completed the little settlement. Until the fifty radio staff moved from Botwood in 1939, there were thirty-eight personnel stationed at Gander. Although far from the sea, the radio staff continued to transmit to the flying boats that used Botwood.

On 11 January, 1938, Fox Moth VO-ADE, owned by Imperial Airways became the first aircraft to land at Gander. It was flown by Captain Douglas Fraser and engineer George Lace, neither of whom later recalled the historic event as anything other than "just a regular ski landing."

But even in 1939 landplanes still did not have the range to fly the ocean, preventing Gander from taking its place on the world's stage. On 15 May, the first aircraft to arrive from abroad (Maine) was a Monocoupe 90A, being flown to Sweden. It left Gander the next day to disappear forever.

Four days later, the largest aircraft to land at Gander were two Handley Page Harrows. These were converted aerial tankers owned by British aviation pioneer, Sir Alan Cobham, and were stationed at Gander to refuel the Imperial Airways flying boats that took-off from Botwood, thus extending their operation through the winter months. On 17 August, a Harrow from Gander successfully refuelled the Imperial Airways flying boat *Cabot* in mid-air: the first such operation over the Atlantic. It was hoped that with the experience gained, trans-Atlantic landplanes would one day also be refuelled in such a manner.

It was the Second World War that made the elaborate and expensive assets of the airport viable. If Europe was to be supplied by air, aircraft would have to be refuelled on islands in the Atlantic. But the most convenient landfalls, Ireland and Portugal, were both neutral, which made the airports at Shannon and in the Azores unavailable. Suddenly, the islands of Newfoundland and Iceland began to assume great importance to the Allied war effort, not only as refuelling stations for aircraft flying to Europe, but also as bases for anti-submarine patrol planes. On 10 February, 1940, two RCAF Lockheed Hudson aircraft from Halifax landed at Gander with a party of senior Canadian military officers. After an inspection tour, they went on to St. John's for discussions with the Newfoundland government on the use of the airport.

This led to an RCAF squadron (10 BR) being stationed at Gander to fly Digbys on anti-submarine patrols. Hangars and cabins were built on the opposite side of the airport to accommodate the squadron. There was some fear that the German military might invade the island, and protection of the RCAF facilities at Gander was given over to the Black Watch Regiment of the Canadian Army, which set up tents and anti-aircraft batteries around the perimeter. As the war progressed, the Digbys were replaced by Cansos, which were themselves replaced by the long-range Liberators — the first aircraft to bridge the Atlantic successfully.

Early in the war, German submarines were sinking Allied cargo vessels with alarming efficiency, and aircraft needed in Europe were becoming too valuable to risk shipping over the Atlantic. So urgent was the need for American-built bombers that London decided to form the Royal Air Force Ferry Command. A string of air bases was to be built in Labrador, Greenland, and Iceland to guide and refuel aircraft directly from American factories to the front in Britain. Initially flown by former Imperial Airways pilots, the aircrews were a ragtag Air Force and civilian group later augmented by graduates from the British Commonwealth Air Training Plan.

The first of the ferry service's flights occurred on 28 October, 1940. A formation of seven Hudson bombers led by Captain Donald C.T. Bennett of British Overseas Airways Corporation, arrived at Gander from Montreal. Canadian Pacific Air Service, tasked with looking after the aircrews, rented two railway sleeping cars and a dining car from the Newfoundland Railway to accommodate them. On 10 November, the Hudsons left Gander and arrived the next morning, without incident, at Aldergrove, Northern Ireland. The Atlantic Ferry was in business. As incredible as this feat was, the lead pilot Bennett later became even more famous for establishing his Pathfinder squadrons.[1]

In early 1941, the United States was still officially neutral, but with German U-boats sinking Allied ships within sight of the American coast, President Roosevelt became increasingly concerned. In May, 1941 a United States Army Air Force reconnaissance squadron arrived at Gander with B-17 Flying Fortress aircraft. The Americans rented hangar space from the RCAF on the far side of the airport, and the US military officially moved in on 8 August. That summer, Gander Lake also became a refuelling stop. On 2 June, the first Catalina to be ferried to England, landed at Gander Lake. On 18 July, it was followed by the more famous Boeing Clipper with a party of VIPs on board. The Americans began their own ferry service through Gander to Prestwick, Scotland, making the airport one of the busiest in the world. The following year, with the American strategic bombing offensive over Germany, hundreds of Flying Fortresses and Liberators were being ferried through Gander. In May 1943, a joint RAF–USAF command post was established in the RAF hangar to coordinate all aircraft ferry movements over the Atlantic.

Trans-Canada Airlines also became a frequent visitor to Gander with their Lockheed 10s, and the administration building was used to process their passengers as Newfoundland was still foreign soil to Canadians. The only other airline to use Gander during the war was British Overseas Airways Corporation (BOAC). So the ferry crews could get back to Dorval and pick up more aircraft, BOAC flew Liberators on the Return Ferry Service (RFS).

By the war's end, the RAF had delivered 6,500 aircraft through Gander, and the US 10,000.[2] The BOAC RFS Liberators had completed 2,000 Atlantic crossings. What had seemed impossible a few years ago was now a daily occurrence. Because so little had been known about polar climatic conditions, or the endurance of aircraft and the crews, there had been a high price to pay. By the war's end, thousands of aircraft taking off from Gander had been lost and over 500 aircrew, including fifty passengers, had died. On board was Major Sir Frederick Banting, one of the discoverers of insulin.

1. Bennett was renown for his navigational skills, which is why he was chosen for the Atlantic Ferry. During World War 2, he set up for Royal Air Force Bomber Command the Pathfinders: aircrews that flew before the main force to locate and mark the target. Bennett's Pathfinders performed acts of unbelievable bravery. One of them was a Canadian, Ian Bazalgette who was awarded the Victoria Cross posthumously. Bazalgette's story is in the author's book *Flying Canucks: Famous Canadian Aviators*, Toronto, Hounslow Press, 1994. For a good book on Bennett's ferry flights see *Ocean Bridge* by Carl Christie, University of Toronto Press, 1995.

2. An enterprising Newfoundlander built a piggery behind the RAF mess, as a form of garbage disposal. With so many VIP flights going through the airport, it became part of the local tour. The piggery owner was Joey Smallwood, the man who would bring Newfoundland into Confederation.

With the end of hostilities in Europe, American, British and Canadian airline operators were quick to realize the potential of Gander. The latest landplanes, such as the DC-4 and Lockheed Constellation, had the range to fly from Gander to Shannon with a passenger payload. In October 1945, DC-4s belonging to American Overseas Airlines and Pan American inaugurated a trans-Atlantic schedule, as did the Constellations of Trans World Airlines and BOAC. As Canadair was still developing the indigenous North Star airliner, Trans-Canada Airlines was forced to use converted Lancaster bombers, called Lancastrian, to begin their Montreal–London run. With the arrival of passengers, the recently vacated air force buildings on both sides of the airport were repainted and pressed into service.

On 1 April 1946 the RAF closed its station and the RCAF officially returned Gander to the government of Newfoundland. The RAF facilities were converted to civil accommodation to become the Skyways Hotel, with its famous Big Dipper bar. In 1946, Gander was as busy as it had been during the war. The Canadian government still had military personnel to be ferried home. On 6 June, the RCAF Lancaster squadrons left Europe for their bases in Canada, flying via Gander.

Gander now entered its glory days and assumed the title Crossroads of the World. All commercial aircraft east- and westbound, landed here, with over 1,000 passengers transiting through it daily. It became a common sight to see the flag carriers of Holland, the United States, Canada, France, Sweden and Britain on the apron at the same time. When Newfoundland joined Canada in 1949, Gander was easily the largest, busiest airport in the country — bringing in an annual revenue of $3 million at a time when the total DOT revenue for all airports was $1.4 million. With the fees collected from the many aircraft refuelling at Gander, the DOT built a terminal building that was opened by Queen Elizabeth in 1959.

The new owners of Gander also created a town for the airport employees, with the streets named after aviation pioneers. Taking the name Gander, it soon had shopping centers, schools and, with the Trans-Canada Highway, developed into a thriving community.

Gander's prosperity came to an end with the introduction of jets on the trans-Atlantic in 1959. The new Boeing 707, Comet 4 and later the DC-8 could fly the Atlantic from New York to London without need of refuelling. The airport was relegated to an "alternate," in case of bad weather, or a stop for charter flights that still used piston-engined aircraft.

But in the 1960s a new group of controversial customers developed. The East Bloc saw Gander as a perfect "technical" stop for refuelling its flights to Cuba and South America. Where once Pan American Stratocruisers had decanted American tourists, now Czech and Interflug Il-62s landed giving their wide-eyed passengers a brief glimpse of the commercial West. For many Communist travellers, Gander was their only hope of defecting. The generosity and kindness shown these refugees by the locals became legendary.

On 25 October, 1967, the Atlantic Ferry Pilot Memorial on Skipper's Drive was unveiled by the man who had led the first of the many Hudson bombers to England in 1940. Still as spry as ever, Air Vice-Marshall D.C.T. Bennett, CB, CBE, DSO, the former Imperial Airways pilot and legendary Pathfinder, returned to Gander to commemorate the thousands of ferry pilots who had used the airport during the war. The Lockheed Hudson Memorial was a joint project of Transport Canada, Eastern Provincial Airlines and Allied Aviation.

Gander celebrated its fiftieth anniversary on 11 January 1988. History had forced many changes upon it. With the fall of the Berlin Wall and the decline in the number of Soviet flights to Cuba, even this source of revenue ended and by 1992 Gander had an annual operating deficit of $4.3 million. The largest passenger aircraft to land at Gander was now a Lockheed L1011, and the airport's two historic runways serve mainly DND, charter and flying school aircraft. As it is part of the National Airport System, federal financial assistance will be phased out by 31 March, 2000.

The Lockheed Hudson Memorial was unveiled in 1967 by Air Vice-Marshall D.C.T. Bennett, of "Pathfinder" fame, to commerate the thousands of ferry pilots that used Gander during the war. (Photo courtesy of Alan Scott, Gander Airport Manager)

Goose Bay

As early as 1939, confronted by a considerably more numerous Luftwaffe than previously thought, the British Air Ministry began putting in orders for aircraft from American manufacturers. Initially, the aircraft, mainly Harvards and Lockheed Hudson bombers, were sent by ship to British ports to be reassembled. The situation changed drastically by 1940, with most of Europe occupied by the Germans and British orders totalling a staggering 26,000 aircraft, to be delivered at 1,000 a month. German U-boats made the Atlantic unsafe for shipping. Then, when a fortunate few ships did make it through, there was considerable delay in unpacking and assembling the bombers.

Although trans-ocean flying was in its infancy, ferrying the aircraft from North America to Britain was the only choice the Allies had. The danger of overflying the Atlantic was obvious to anyone associated with aviation. The ocean was thought impossible to fly over in winter, as aircraft did not have the fuel to complete the full crossing and there were no emergency airfields, radio aids, or even the possi-

bility of rescue should the pilot have to ditch. But by 1940, the British, French and Dutch aircraft orders were beginning to be backlogged in great quantities at American and Canadian airports, so much so that President Roosevelt began to question their urgency.

Desperate for the aircraft, the British insisted the planes be flown over. Organized by Canadian Pacific Airlines, the ferry flights from Gander to Prestwick, Scotland, began in November 1940. However, as innovative as this was, the number of aircraft delivered through Newfoundland were still too few to make much difference in the backlog. By early 1941, the British and Canadian governments began looking into revamping their ferrying operations by constructing a string of weather stations and airstrips from Montreal to Britain. The British already had refuelling bases at Gander, Newfoundland and Reykjavik, Iceland, but alternate routes in case of bad weather were needed. For its part, the Canadian government surveyed northern Quebec and Labrador for possible airfields.

A second reason for more bases was that a shorter route would be more suitable for smaller aircraft like fighters. The Battle of Britain emphasized the high attrition rate of fighter aircraft in the war, but Gander and Reykjavik were still too far apart for fighters to be ferried across. If they could be flown via Labrador, Greenland and Iceland, they would have more of a chance of making it. Then too, an air route over those land masses would mean less time spent over the icy Atlantic.

Although still neutral, in early 1941 the Americans established a protectorate over Greenland and carved out an airport at Narssarssuaq. In June 1941, with the permission of the government of Newfoundland, the RCAF sent a photographic unit and a survey team from the Department of Mines and Resources to the wilderness of Labrador. The need for an airport in this remote region was becoming all the more urgent, as the Allies felt that without some sort of RCAF presence, the Germans could set up a U-boat base in one of the many Labrador bays with impunity. So vital was a ferry airport in Labrador to the war effort that Ottawa budgeted $20 million for its construction.

As the early bush pilots knew, it proved more difficult to fly into Labrador than the RCAF thought. Although it was summer, the Air Force Stranraer flying boat transporting the team to the Hamilton River basin was forced back, because of snow and freezing rain. The pilot put down in one of the outports where, because of wind-driven ice, the party was stranded for ten days.

Later flights over the Northwest River were more successful and a site was chosen. Eric Fry of the Topographical Survey is credited with first seeing the plateau on Hamilton Inlet at the mouth of the Goose River. The party landed, and made sure there was a supply of sand, gravel and timber nearby for construction of runways and a navigable outlet to the ocean for supply ships. Because ice would prevent any navigation as early as October, on 17 September 1941 the first of the chartered ships arrived at Goose Bay with men, machinery and supplies. A wharf was built on 23 September and soon three runways were laid out. By 7 December, aircraft began flying in.

As Goose was only accessible by water during the summer, the RCAF took over responsibility for the freighting of men, food and fuel through the long winter. By the time the United States entered the war, the airport was fully operational. By July 1942, the stream of British and Canadian ferried aircraft had been eclipsed by the more than 650 fighters and bombers of the United States Eighth Air Force landing and refueling on their way to British bases. So close were the ferry airports now, the trans-Atlantic route could be flown by relatively inexperienced operational pilots rather than the ferry ones.

Using first Lockheed Lodestars and later Douglas C-47s, RCAF 164 (Transport) Squadron began flying in 663,200 pounds (298,440 kilograms) of freight for the first winter at Goose Bay. Family homes were built in the area known as Happy Valley, and air defence was provided by the Hurricanes of 129 Squadron RCAF.

At the end of the war, the RCAF decided to continue its lease (Goose Bay still being in a foreign country), and Trans-Canada Airlines began to fly its North Stars through it on scheduled services to Europe. The RCAF was persuaded to give up part of its hangar for the first passenger terminal, and it was hoped other airlines would transfer from the crowded facilities at Gander Airport. But the Newfoundland government, with the most to lose if air traffic was diverted from Gander, dissuaded the Canadian and American authorities from using Goose Bay to its full potential, keeping it only as an alternate to Gander.

It took the Cold War to give isolated Goose Bay a new lease on life. The United States made it an integral part of the North American air defense shield, stationing Strategic Air Command tanker aircraft at permanent readiness on its apron. Although it was still technically an RCAF base, the USAF strengthened and extended the runways, built married quarters, and a hospital; by 1959 there were over 3,000 Americans living at the base.

The airport welcomed another wartime customer in 1967, when the RAF arrived to carry out low-level training flights over Labrador (the terrain being much like that of the Soviet Union) and rotated first Vulcan and then Tornado bombers through Goose Bay.

In 1978, Transport Canada took over the maintenance of Goose Bay from the RCAF. It built a new air terminal building, but DND continued to operate the control tower and maintenance garage. With the end of the Cold War, the Canadian government began to cast around for a role for the airport. No longer relevant to commercial air routes, Goose Bay began to specialise in renting its facilities and terrain for low-level fighter training. This was especially attractive to Canada's NATO partners whose air forces were increasingly forced to curtail their sorties in the crowded skies at home.

In 1986, the Dutch, German and British governments negotiated a ten year lease for fighter training operations at Goose Bay, paying $12,000 per sortie as their share of infrastructure costs. A public awareness campaign forced Ottawa to take the environmental concerns of the native people in Labrador into account. In response, the DND set up an Institute of Environmental Monitoring and Research to monitor the impact of the low-level flights. At first Ottawa only allowed 7,300 sorties to be flown by the "guests" annually, but in June 1995 the total was raised to 18,000. The Belgian and Italian air forces have also expressed interest in deploying to the airport. The Goose Bay project office hoped other potential customers might include Eastern European air forces under NATO's Partnership for Peace program.

The airport's future may have actually been decided not in Europe but closer to home. Voisey Bay, the site of the largest nickel find in thirty years, is barely 300 miles (483 kilometres) away. Goose is perfectly positioned to become the support base for the mining companies. The boom caused the old facilities at the airport to be renovated and expanded. Hotels, shopping centres and schools were planned for the expected influx of miners and their families. Air Labrador and Canadian Helicopters Corp. both saw their flights out of Goose Bay increase by forty per cent.

Today Goose is served by five scheduled air carriers, with the largest aircraft to use it a Boeing 737. The airport incurred a deficit of $617,095 in 1992 and, as federal financial aid will be phased out by 31 March 2000, the revenue from low-flying flights and the mining boom will begin to look more attractive. As a monument to the airport's historic purpose when it served as a bomber ferry base, a Royal Air Force Vulcan sits outside CFB Goose Bay.

Halifax

Flying in the Halifax area began at the Nova Scotia Exhibition of 1912. From 11 September to the 20th, American Charles F. Walsh flew daily circuits over the exhibition grounds. He also became the first to fly over the city of Halifax and almost lost his life doing so. One of his aircraft was wrecked on the fence at the fairground's edge and later, attempting to take off in another plane, he narrowly missed first the cow barns, then the telegraph wires and finally a stationary locomotive on a railway siding. On the final day of the exhibition, Walsh took off without mishap, but on landing smashed into a board fence at the edge of the field, completely destroying the aircraft.[1] Such were the perils of not having proper airfields.

During the First World War, the port of Halifax became the North American assembly point for Atlantic convoys. Fearful of the new long range German submarines, the British and United States governments asked that the har-bour's approaches be patrolled by seaplanes. When in 1918, a U-boat torpedoed and sank an oil tanker within ten miles (16 kilometres) of Halifax harbour, Ottawa belatedly formed the Royal Canadian Naval Air Service to be stationed at Baker's Point, near Dartmouth. While the Canadian pilots were being trained, the United States, then sending large concentrations of troops through Halifax, moved a US Navy Flying Corps detachment to the Point. In August, 1918 the Americans began operating Curtiss HS-2L flying boats over the convoys.[2] Before the Canadians could complete their training the war ended and the United States Navy left, after turning their aircraft over to Canada. The Curtiss flying boats were stored at Dartmouth Air Station until they could be used either by the Air Board or provincial governments.

The City of Halifax began lobbying the federal government for an airport as early as 1919, but it was a decade

---

1. Walsh was living on borrowed time: his luck ran out thirteen days later when he was killed trying to land at a demonstration at Trenton, New Jersey.

2. One of the U.S. Navy pilots based at Halifax was Richard E. Byrd, the future polar aviator.

The original Halifax airport on Chebucto Road, bounded by Mumford Road and Connaught Avenue, in the early 1930s. (Public Archives of Nova Scotia N-4407)

before the Civil Aviation Branch of the Department of National Defence promised to assist. A site was chosen at Bluebell Farm and two runways of 1,812 by 610 feet (549 by 183 metres) and 2,013 by 610 feet (610 by 183 metres) were laid out. In February 1931, the first aircraft landed at Halifax Airport. Today, outlines of this first airport can be traced at Saunders Park near the Westmount housing estate on Chebucto Road. The airport's first users were air companies from below the border and the Halifax Aero Club.

With the Depression, all airmail contracts dwindled and the only aircraft to use the new airport regularly belonged to Pan American Airways on their run to Boston. The RCAF built an air base at Shearwater and when the Second World War began, patrolled the harbour approaches with Digby bombers.

Trans-Canada Airlines used Shearwater airport until 1960. In 1941, with convoys once more massing in the

Pan American Airways pilot Rod Sullivan in front of his twin-engine Sikorsky amphibian at the Chebucto Road airport in 1931. The plane on the Boston—Halifax route carried eight passengers, with stops in Saint John, New Brunswick and Calais, Bangor, Rockland, and Portland, Maine. (Public Archives of Nova Scotia N-4403)

harbour and thousands of troops being shipped overseas, the airport was closed down and turned into an army camp.

After the war the search for a purely civil airport began. In 1954, Trans-Canada Airlines recommended a site near Kelly's Lake. A terminal building and two runways 8,000 by 200 feet (2,439 by 61 metres) and 6,200 by 200 feet (1,890 by 61 metres) were constructed and the airport was opened on Canada Day 1960. Halifax became the "alternate" for American and Canadian airports. At a time when bad weather could close New York or Boston, Halifax suddenly found itself inundated with trans-Atlantic flights.

Because of this, the airport restaurants and bars could be counted on to remain open very late, a fact not lost on the local young men.

Today, Halifax International Airport is served by eight scheduled carriers, the largest aircraft to use it is Air Canada's Boeing 767-300. In 1992, 2.5 million passengers passed through it and the airport was operated at a considerable financial surplus. As a National Airport System (NAS) airport, it is scheduled to be transferred under a long term lease to a local airport authority.

When bad weather closed the airports at Boston and New York, Halifax would be inundated with re-directed flights. This terminal at Kelly's Lake was opened on Canada Day, 1960. (Air Canada Archives)

Hamilton

With Montreal and Toronto, Hamilton had its share of the pre-World War I air meets. The Niagara area was a popular recreation spot for Torontonians, and thus a magnet for exhibition flyers who earned their living by playing before large audiences. On 27 July 1911, a field near Tuckett's Farm on Beach Road became the venue for the Hamilton air meet sponsored by local businessmen. When it ended on 2 August, the sponsors staged the country's first air race, from Hamilton to Toronto. Charles Willard, an American aviator, and John A.D. McCurdy of Baddeck, Nova Scotia were two of the more famous competitors who took-off from Tuckett's Farm. McCurdy won, flying the thirty-five miles (56 kilometres) in thirty-six minutes and landing on Toronto Island. Willard, only a few minutes behind, landed at the Exhibition Grounds.

Unfortunately, Hamilton, like Quebec City, suffered from its proximity to a larger urban area: in this case Toronto, where in the 1920s there were five airfields in operation. It would not be until 1926 that Hamilton's first airport was opened and that by a local entrepreneur. Jack V. Elliot started his own aviation school on Burlington Beach Road, near Stewart Park. Elliot was a colourful character with an eye for what the public wanted. He began selling automobile accessories during World War I. When the business prospered, he sold it to finance Hamilton's first radio station, CFCU. Elliot also developed a passion for speed boats and became the commodore of the Hamilton Boat Club.

There are many stories about how he came into aviation. In one version, two Curtiss Jennies (still crated) were delivered to him in lieu of a debt repayment. Although he knew nothing about aircraft, Elliot had the Jennies assembled, and set about recouping his losses by using them as flying billboards and then as trainers for a flying school. Elliot had heard it was then the policy of the federal government to teach anyone who owned an aircraft to fly, and he immediately took lessons at Camp Borden to teach others as well. Another version has it that Elliot bought a

Hamilton's first airport was a flying school set up in the 1920s by local businessman Jack Elliot. Eileen Vollick, the first Canadian woman to earn her pilot's licence was one of his students. (National Archives of Canada C61597)

Curtiss Jenny to fly over the 1922 Gold Cup Races for Motor Boats in Hamilton harbour to impress the editor of New York's *Motor Boating* magazine.

Two of Elliot's pupils were Walt Fowler, one of the first pilots for Trans-Canada Airlines, and Frank Young who would be awarded the Trans-Canada Trophy thirty years later. But the most famous of the students was Eileen M. Vollick, the first woman to receive a private pilot's licence

in Canada. All recalled their days at the Jack Elliot Flying School with some affection. Students were forced to dress in war-surplus military uniforms (Elliot had bought hundreds very cheaply) complete with puttees and were charged a dollar a minute for flights.

There are also different stories about how Elliot built his hangars. In one, he purchased thousands of war-surplus propellers for three cents each. Using the packing crates the propellers came in, he collected enough wood to build his own hangar, naming the airport after himself. More than likely, he went to Beamsville, the site of the wartime RFC flying school, and had one of the disused hangars disassembled and re-erected at his airport. As Elliot Airport was on Burlington Beach, in the winter the frozen lake was used. Ever the businessman, in 1927 Elliot tried to convince the City of Hamilton to build an airport that he and the city could use. While Mayor Treleaven was in favour of the idea, he was outvoted by others on the Board of Control. In 1928, International Airways bought out the flamboyant Elliot, and he retired to run a trailer park in Houston, Texas. Hamilton's aviation pioneer died there on 30 September, 1964 at the age of seventy-one.

In 1927, when the Department of Defence announced its Flying Club Scheme — that it would provide financial assistance to any flying club that maintained an airfield — Hamilton's Board of Control was the first to apply. It seemed a cheap way of getting a municipal airport with federal funds. The following year the city, perhaps recalling Elliot's offer, acquired a site two kilometres (1.24 miles) south of Elliot's school for its municipal airport. Three runways were laid out and the Civic Airport opened on 6 June, 1929.

In March 1930, the Post Office awarded an airmail contract to Canadian Airways, the new owners of International Airways which used Hamilton Airport on their Detroit to Toronto route. The timing was unfortunate as Hamilton was beginning to encounter the difficulties of the Depression. It was suddenly faced with paving the new airport's runways, installing field lighting and a rotating beacon. By the time the work was completed a year later, Prime Minister R.B. Bennett cancelled all airmail contracts and Canadian Airways left partially completed Hamilton Airport to its debts.

However, the site did achieve some fame as the location of the first Trans-Canada Air Pageant. Organized by the Canadian Flying Clubs Association to stimulate public interest in aviation, twenty aircraft and an RCAF flight toured the country in 1931. They took off from Hamilton on Canada Day, July 1, stopping at all the main cities as far as Vancouver, then retracing their routes to the Maritimes before returning home. Along the way, twenty-six shows were performed before audiences who had hardly seen a single aircraft, let alone so many in RCAF colours.

Through the darkest days of the Depression the only tenant at the airport was the Hamilton Aero Club, and the City begged for maintenance grants from the federal government, but in vain. In 1937, it lobbied unsuccessfully for the new Trans-Canada Airlines to serve Hamilton after Toronto. The Department of Transport thought the region was well served by airports at Malton and Toronto Harbour.

In 1939, when World War II began, Hamilton, like many other cities, pressured the Department of National Defence to have a flying training school set up at the airport. After all, the need for airports for the British Commonwealth Air Training Plan (BCATP) was so desperate, it was reported the Minister for Munitions C.D. Howe was even planning to use the isolated airfields of the Trans-Canada Airway. But once more its hopes were dashed. The military decided to build an airport for the BCATP at Mount Hope, southwest of the city. In 1943 when the Hamilton Aero Club transferred to the new Mount Hope Airport, the municipal airport's only tenant was the Cub Aircraft factory.

Other companies joined Cub at the airport after the war. They were Narvy Aircraft, Warriors Air Services, Peninsula Air Services and finally Trans Aircraft Ltd. But by then the runways had deteriorated to a dangerous level and the city had crept up around the airport. After battling the Depression and the military, Hamilton Municipal Airport finally closed in November 1951.

Mount Hope Airport

In 1940, a military survey team thought that Hamilton Municipal Airport was too small for the air schools of the British Commonwealth Air Training Plan and built an airport at Mount Hope, southwest of Hamilton. Here under the Hamilton Aero Club, No. 10 Flying Training School was established, sharing the airport with the RAF Air Navigation School.

After the war, the Department of Transport took over operation of the Airport, which although still unlicensed was used by the RCAF and the Hamilton Aero Club. The RCAF moved out in 1962 and several air companies transferred over from the municipal airport. In 1961, Nordair linked Hamilton with Toronto, Oshawa, Kingston and Montreal, along what was called its Seaway Route. This encouraged the City of Hamilton to hope other airlines might join it and use the airport, and in 1964 it leased the property from the DOT.

In 1969, a new terminal building was constructed and in a bid to attract airlines from Toronto's Pearson Airport, 150 acres (60 hectares) from the neighbouring golf course were developed. A new terminal and control tower were built in 1984.

In 1940, the federal government built Mount Hope Airport for the flying schools of the British Commonwealth Air Training Plan. The BCATP hangars are still in use today. (Hamilton Airport photo)

In 1973, the Canadian Warplane Heritage took over some of the old BCATP hangars for the restoration and display of vintage aircraft. In February 1993, a disastrous fire in the restoration hangar destroyed its Hawker Hurricane and Supermarine Spitfire but, fortunately, not North America's only flying Lancaster bomber. The museum's supporters with thousands of Canadians, rallied around to help the CWH maintain the remaining aircraft in temporary quarters. Through their effort, a permanent home in the form of a delta-shaped 108,000 square foot (9,720 square metre) museum complex was begun by the entrance to the airport. The completion date is set for spring, 1996.

Without a nightly curfew, Hamilton Airport comes alive at night as the air cargo centre for Southern Ontario. As there is no congestion in the air, or on the ground, cargo jets (mainly Boeing 727s) land and take-off from its runways throughout the night. On one particularly busy night in January, 1995, fifty-eight freighters landed between 11 P.M. and 7 A.M. to unload, reload and take-off. The night flying restrictions at Pearson International, coupled with its political problems, can only help Hamilton Airport's cause.

But it has been unsuccessful in luring passengers away from Toronto or Buffalo airports. Although Hamilton's terminal has the potential for handling 600 flights a week, its present quota of forty-two (mainly US Air and Air Laurentian) hardly impact on its facilities at all.

One of the reasons might be that passengers are reluctant to use an airport with poor access to Highway 403, the main thoroughfare in the region. If an expressway linking the airport with the highway is a priority, another might be a public relations program to convince small airlines to use what could become Toronto's second airport. Both London and New York are ringed with airports that siphon the congestion off each other. The ongoing problems of both Toronto Island Airport and Pearson International might still work to Hamilton's advantage.

Under the National Airport Policy, Hamilton Airport will be sold to provincial, regional and private interests. A Strategic Study commissioned by the regional municipality has recommended that the Hamilton–Wentworth region assume ownership of the airport. If Hamilton can become Toronto's second airport, the study calculates that it will move from an annual deficit of $1 million to a net surplus of $4.8 million. One cannot help feeling that Jack Elliot would have approved.

A fire swept through the Canadian Warplane Heritage restoration hangar in February 1993, destroying its Hawker Hurricane and Supermarine Spitfire. A new permanent home is scheduled to open in the spring of 1996. (Hamilton Airport photo)

Airports of the Montreal Region

At the start of this century, as citizens of the largest, wealthiest city in Canada, Montrealers took it as their right to be in the forefront of aviation. On 2 July 1910, French aviator Count Jacques De Lesseps flying *Le Scarabée*, a Bleriot monoplane, did a wide circuit over Montreal for forty-five minutes, the first time a Canadian city had been flown over.

He was taking part in the Great Montreal Air Meet. The meet was the brainchild of John Bassett, then a young reporter for the now defunct Montreal newspaper *The Daily Witness*. Displaying the skills in public relations that would soon make him a millionaire, Bassett convinced the Royal Automobile Club of Canada and the Montreal Tramways to sponsor the event. For eight days that summer in 1910, the farms at Lakeside on the West Island became the centre of aviation in North America, as more than a hundred aircraft and 20,000 spectators assembled there for the Air Meet. There were airships as well; one of the most spectacular was the Knabenshue airship flown by Cromwell Dixon. But their sausage shapes already seemed part of the previous century, and this one definitely belonged to the flying machines. The Lakeside meet was a competition between the pilots of two continents, the Europeans in their Bleriot monoplanes and the North Americans using Wright biplanes — both struggling to establish supremacy in the air.

On what became the first airfield in Canada, albeit a temporary one, land was cleared, ditches filled in and bleachers erected to accommodate the aviators and their crowds of supporters. Admission ranged from fifty cents to $2 and twenty special trains carried spectators to Lakeside. Among those present that day were some who would become famous in Canadian aviation in years to come: J.A.D. McCurdy, Walter Brookins and a very young Walter Gilbert.

Once the Air Meet ended, the aviators dismantled their craft and moved on to the second meet in Toronto, leaving Lakeside to its obscurity once more. But aircraft continued to fly from other fields around Montreal. King Edward Park, downtown, was used by De Lesseps as a landing field on his return from Toronto. A fairground promoter would later buy one of the Count's Bleriots and put it on display there.

On 8 October 1913, William Robinson took off for Ottawa at 9:50 A.M. from Snowdon Junction in a Lillie biplane. He carried copies of that day's *Daily Mail* newspaper for Prime Minister Sir Robert Borden and Sir Wilfrid Laurier. A broken fuel line forced him down at Lachine, almost where the runways of Dorval Airport are today. A local mechanic fixed his plane and Robinson took off once more, following the Canadian Pacific Railway lines to Ottawa. His other stops were Rigaud, Caledonia Springs and Leonard, and he arrived in Ottawa at 5:00 P.M. He had hoped to put down at Lansdowne Park, but because of the crowds of people who had come out to watch him, Robinson was forced to land at a nearby cow pasture called Slattery's Field.

In June 1918, Captain Brian Peck of the RAF flew the first official airmail service from the Bois de Boulogne race track in Montreal to Leaside in Toronto.

Cartierville

The first authentic airfield in Montreal was laid out on the polo grounds on the corner of Bois Franc Road (now Blvd. Henri Bourassa) and Montee St. Laurent (now Blvd. Laurentian). The closest village was Cartierville, where Gervais Cousineau leased some land to young Percy Reid. Reid experimented with his home-made aircraft and actually made a short hop in it on 7 July 1911. At first he stored his plane in Cousineau's barn, but in 1913 built his own hangar — the first ever constructed in Canada. Unfortunately a windstorm destroyed it in October.[1] After the First World War, Reid went into partnership with the Curtiss Company to manufacture their aircraft. His Curtiss–Reid Rambler became a common sight at air clubs across Canada for many years. In 1920, the Aerial League of the British Empire was given a licence to operate an airport at Cartierville.

There were other airfields and air harbours scattered around the city: the Vickers aircraft factory near the docks, small airfields at Lasalle, Pointe aux Trembles and across the river at Longueuil. Some would disappear under the encroachment of suburbia but Cartierville would remain,

---

1. Reid had the worst luck with hangars at that location. On 17 May 1930 and on 24 September 1942, windstorms struck the exact spot and levelled hangars built there.

The Second World War transformed airports into industrial complexes that rivalled the shipyards. Some 2,800 Harvards were built at Cartierville by Noorduyn. This one is maintained by Canadian Warplane Heritage. (Author's photo)

becoming first the factory airport for the Curtiss–Reid Company, then Noorduyn and Canadian Vickers and finally Canadair.

In 1934, the Dutch aircraft designer Bob Noorduyn opened Noorduyn Aircraft Ltd. in the old Curtiss–Reid facilities. Here he built 2,800 Norseman planes, that uniquely Canadian aircraft, beloved of bush pilots and still flying today. During and after the Second World War, Noorduyn's factory thrived as it manufactured Havard trainers and Canso patrol aircraft. Noorduyn built its own factory on Bois Franc Road and Federal Aircraft leased the old Curtiss–Reid plant to build Ansons. In 1943, Federal sold its lease to Canadian Car and Foundry, which made the unusual Burnelli CBY-3 Loadmaster prototype in 1945.

Across the runway from Noorduyn, Canadian Vickers built a plant on Blvd. Laurentien in 1943 to turn out Consolidated PBY patrol bombers. The following year, Vickers left the aircraft manufacturing business and sold their factory to a group of businessmen who formed Canadair Ltd. With capital raised from the Electric Boat Company, Canadair expanded and bought 657,000 feet (200,254 metres) along Blvd. Laurentian, at six cents a foot, to re-build the factory.

At first it continued making Vickers aircraft from spare parts, then shifted to converting the hundreds of war-surplus DC-3s to civilian use. The capital raised by these enterprises meant that Canadair could design and build its own aircraft. On 15 July 1946, the Canadair North Star took-off from Cartierville on a twenty-five minute flight. In the years that followed, Canadair would make the Argus, the Yukon, fighter aircraft and water bombers. But it was the success of the North Star that gave it, and Cartierville, a future. So busy did it become that by 1970 all general aviation was transferred away from Cartierville, leaving it entirely for Canadair.

This 1950s aerial photo of Cartierville captures its history well. Still visible, where Blvds. Laurentian and St. Laurent intersect, is the workshop built by Percy Reid in 1913. Flanked by the giant Canadair plant on the right and the Noorduyn factory below, the scene symbolizes the evolution of aviation in Canada. (Canadair D-6093)

With the opening of the Canadair building at Dorval in 1993, all flying ceased at Cartierville and it was developed as a housing estate. In 1995, there were several streets of homes built on land where much of Canada's aviation history had taken place. There remains no monument to mark where Percy Reid flew, where Noorduyn produced Harvards and where C.D. Howe's North Stars took to the air. Sadly, the passing of Canada's oldest, continuously operating airport was ignored by the nation it served so well.

Longueuil

In the 1920s, Fairchild Aircraft Co. operated a public seaplane base and a private airport, on the shores of the St. Lawrence at Longueuil, opposite Green Island. The airport had four runways laid out as the spokes of a wheel for aircraft to land or take-off in any direction. Here Fairchild built the FC-71 and the "razor-back" FC-2. Longueuil's river moorings came to media attention in 1937 as the Canadian seaplane base for Britain's Imperial Airways. The Imperial Airways flying boat *Caribou* inaugurated a weekly trans-Atlantic service in 1939, connecting Southampton with Montreal. However, this was the last of civil flying boats on the St. Lawrence River. During the Second World

War some flying boats did land at Boucherville, northeast of Longueuil, but these were flown by the Royal Air Force.

St. Hubert

At the Imperial Conference in London in 1926, Britain and her Dominions agreed that the Empire would be better held together by mammoth airships plying between the mother country and the colonies. As the major industrial power, Britain would build the airships and the Dominions would provide the ground facilities for their servicing. Canada agreed to build a mooring base for the trans-Atlantic terminus of the route, and in 1927 two British Air Ministry officials were sent to Montreal to select a site. They decided on an area eight miles (13 kilometres) from the Longueuil airport in the municipality of St. Hubert. This suited Ottawa, as the federal government was actively searching for a base for airmail flights and accepted that a federally owned and operated airport at St. Hubert was an idea whose time had come.

Delivering letters by aircraft had long been underway in Europe and the United States, and the Canadian postal authorities were eager to provide a similar service. If there was little that could be done to speed up mail across the Atlantic, at least ships could be met as far offshore as possible and the mail taken off them by seaplanes for

A good aerial view of the first airport in Canada, St. Hubert, Quebec, 1930, with the R-100 airship tethered to the mooring tower. The tents in the bottom left belong to military units sent to control the crowds that flocked to see the R-100. (National Archives of Canada PA 117691)

delivery inland. This imaginative solution was actually implemented. At this time, ships entering the St. Lawrence River were met by the pilot boat off Father Point, close to the city of Rimouski, Quebec. On 9 September, 1927 John Henry (Tuddy) Tudhope landed alongside the liner *Empress of France* off Father Point. He transferred its mail bags to his Vickers Vanessa floatplane and flew to Rimouski, and then on to Montreal.

But although subsequent flights to incoming ships were carried out through the fall of 1927, landing near an ocean liner and throwing mail bags into a pitching aircraft was dangerous in any weather and impossible in the winter. There were also no sheltered harbours along this area of the St. Lawrence for a seaplane to be based in. If a reliable system was to be developed, more permanent, fixed facilities on land were necessary. The Post Office's solution was to have the pilot boat take the bags to Rimouski, where an airfield could be built so they would be flown to St. Hubert.

In June 1927, the federal government took the unprecedented step of constructing and operating airports at Rimouski and St. Hubert for its airmail route. Mail flown to St. Hubert was re-bagged for the Canadian Airways flight for Toronto and the Colonial Airways' flight to Albany, New York. At St. Hubert, even as the airship mooring base was being built, runways were measured out and a hangar erected. In November, the first aircraft to use the airport was a Fairchild owned by the military. Two hard-surfaced runways were constructed under the supervision of the engineering firm of Messers. Corriveau, Adam and Dansereau. Because of the airmail, a rotating beacon and runway lighting were installed for night flights.

As the North American base for the British airships, St. Hubert's most prominent feature was the mooring tower. This was a marvel of the era and deserves closer examination. The mast was 210 feet (64 metres) high and had a system of elevators to carry the passengers and food to the airship. The control cabin on the mast was thirty-eight feet (12 metres) in diameter and shipped intact from England. At the base of the mast were waiting rooms, two hydrogen generating plants and a large gasoline tank. The gasoline was fed to the airship's fuel tanks under water pressure. Three electrical winches provided the power to move the tower and align it to the nose of the airship, in an intricate docking procedure. Ottawa provided a well-equipped radio room and a detachment of operators from the Royal Canadian Corps of Signallers to guide the airship in. There was even a weather office from the Department of Marine to give reports and forecasts.

On 1 August 1930 at 1:30 A.M., the R-100 airship docked at St. Hubert. It had taken seventy-eight hours and fifty-two minutes to cross the Atlantic. The appearance of the R-100 caused a sensation in Montreal, and hundreds of cars and special trains brought an estimated one million spectators to the airport. With a length of 689 feet (208.6 metres), the sausage shaped aircraft tethered to the mast was visible from far across the countryside. On 10 August, the airship set off for a leisurely tour over Montreal, Ottawa, Toronto and Niagara Falls. When it returned via St. Hubert to England on the 13th, who could doubt that the Age of the Airship had arrived?

St. Hubert basked in the publicity of the R-100's visit. Over 3,000 aircraft landed while it was there and everyone from the Minister of Defence, J.L. Ralston, to Camillien Houde, the Mayor of Montreal managed to pay a visit to the airport. But when news came on 4 October that the R-100's sistership crashed and burned on its way to India, the great imperial airship route was given up.[2] The mooring tower became a hazard to the airmail flights and was demolished for scrap in 1938. Its concrete base, at the end of Runway 18-36, is all that remains today of what might have been.

Perhaps because of the fear of fire from the airships, in 1930 the federal government provided St. Hubert with a fire engine and fire hall: making it the first Canadian civil airport to have fully-manned fire services.

During the Depression, the airmail routes were cancelled, and it would not be until 1936 that the Department of Transport began reinvesting in St. Hubert by building more runways and hangars. On 30 July 1937, a group of distinguished Canadian aviators gathered at St. Hubert for a historic dusk-to-dawn flight from Montreal to Vancouver along the Trans-Canada Airway. Among them was C.D. Howe, the Minister for Transport. The Lockheed being used was flown by Tuddy Tudhope, a decade after he had met ocean liners in the St. Lawrence. One of the many stories that came out of the flight was that when the aircraft was buffeted by severe turbulence through the Rockies, everyone except the Minister became apprehensive. As the survivor of many a battle in the House of Commons, Howe placidly read his papers and puffed on his pipe. The St. Hubert flight went a long way to prove that the Trans-Canada Airway was a success.

With more airlines using the airport, the airspace around St. Hubert became busier, and early air traffic control was begun. Curt Bogart, an air inspector from the DOT, was selected to become Canada's first air traffic controller and was sent to Newark, New Jersey for training. He re-

2. So deeply did the airship disaster affect the nation, that flags across Canada were flown at half-mast

turned to St. Hubert in February 1939, opening Canada's first control tower on 13 April.

On 1 April 1939, another Trans-Canada Airlines Lockheed lifted off the runway at St. Hubert, bound for Vancouver. The flight would take sixteen hours flying time, and stops would be made at Toronto, Winnipeg and Lethbridge. Unlike the flight two years before, this was the first commercial transcontinental flight across Canada with paying passengers. On 2 April an eastbound TCA aircraft from Vancouver arrived at St. Hubert.

During the War, the DND took over administration of the airport, intending to use it for aircrew training. Then in September, 1940 the first of hundreds of Lockheed Hudson bombers landed at the airport. Like Gander, St. Hubert was well-equipped, with its runways, lighting and radio equipment, to cope with the ferrying of much needed aircraft to England. The Ferry Command operation, initially run by Canadian Pacific Railway, made St. Hubert the assembly point of all aircraft to be ferried to Britain. The Allies had placed huge orders for bombers from American companies, and dismantling them to be shipped over U-boat infested waters was proving to be too risky. As the United States was still officially neutral, the aircraft were flown from American factories to Pembina, North Dakota, then dragged across the Canadian border by tractor and flown to St. Hubert.

There all modifications were carried out on the bombers for military service in the RAF. Imperial Airways staff who had experience with trans-Atlantic flying set about training the crews. To alleviate the shortage of competent civilian pilots, a princely salary ($1,000 a month) was offered to pilots with long distance flying experience, and many American and neutral soldiers of fortune signed up. In February, 1941 C.H. (Punch) Dickins, the veteran bush pilot, arrived at St. Hubert to take over the Ferry operation as general manager.

By the time the Canadian Pacific contract was terminated on 20 July, 1941 and the Royal Air Force took over, 289 aircraft, mainly Hudsons and a few Flying Fortresses, had been flown through St. Hubert to Gander and England. Flights that would have merited world-wide media coverage a few years ago, had become routine, or as routine as it was possible to make them. But the airport, with its BCATP flying school and ferrying operations, was becoming too crowded. On 1 September 1941, the Atlantic Ferry Command and all the airlines were transferred to newly built Dorval Airport. St. Hubert became exclusively an RCAF airbase and after the war the Canadian headquarters for the North American Air Defence Command.

United Aircraft, manufacturing Pratt & Whitney aircraft engines, moved to St. Hubert from St. Jean Airport in 1965 and constructed a large factory with access to the runway. The distinctive Boeing 720 it used as a test bed for its engines, soon became a familiar sight at the airport.

By 1968, although the Department of National Defence was still actively involved in St. Hubert, Transport Canada once more took over operations in preparation for the airport's new role in the general aviation sector. In 1970 all general aviation from Cartierville was transferred to the airport. New administration and maintenance buildings were erected and in 1985, two years before St. Hubert was to celebrate its fiftieth anniversary, a $2.2 million control tower was built.

The airport is home to United Aircraft, several flying schools, the Montreal Flying Club, a military base, and corporate and private aviation. St. Hubert was designated a satellite airport to Mirabel and Dorval and offered for transfer to the Aeroports de Montréal.

Dorval

Two miles (3.2 kilometres) from where the Lakeside Air Meet had taken place, was the village of Dorval. It had a racetrack, complete with jockey club, and its own railroad siding. In 1940, the racetrack was bought by the Department of Transport as the site for an airport to alleviate the wartime congestion at St. Hubert. The field was well sited near the Dorval train station and only a few miles from Lachine, one of the giant manning depots for the RCAF.

By 2 September 1941, two 5,000 feet (1,524 metres) runways had been laid, and all commercial operations and the Ferry Command were moved over from St. Hubert. The air terminal building was ready by December and, unlike the clapboard terminal at Malton, was a substantial two storey structure built in masonry and plate glass with a control tower. Its main hall and huge passenger lounge, looked out on the ramp. The whole building was arced around a circular car park with maintenance hangars on the side. The Royal Bank opened a branch within the terminal and Canadian Railway News provided the catering for the trans-Atlantic flights.

Some of the ferry crews were billeted in a barrack-like structure called the Airport Inn, the more fortunate driven by Murray Hill bus to the Mont Royal Hotel in Montreal. Throughout the war, the tarmac at Dorval resembled nothing more than a mechanical version of a beehive, with aircraft being delivered from Burbank, California, to be modified and then flown on familiarisation flights. The ferry crews finally took them over and, with RAF roundels painted on, they lumbered down Dorval's runway loaded with fuel for the long flight to Gander and eventually Prestwick in Scotland.

Local residents remember that there were always a few burnt-out wrecks on the airport's perimeter, as the pilots attempted to cope with bombers that had been rushed through their manufacturing and testing stages for delivery. The pilots who flew the Mitchells and Liberators were relieved that RAF Ferry Command operated its own crash-fire service at Dorval. Later in the war, a quasi form of airline began at the airport when the Canadian Government Trans Atlantic Air Service (CGTAS) and BOAC operated regular passenger flights using Lancasters and Liberators respectively.

On 17 September 1945, the first Lockheed Constellation landed at Dorval. It proceeded to fly demonstration flights over Montreal, heralding the end of the war and the start of civilian operations. The RAF closed down its ferry services in 1945, and a year later the RCAF handed the management of Dorval Airport over to the DOT, although because of RCAF Station Lachine, it retained some hangars and offices for flight movements.

In March, 1947, 426 Squadron RCAF made Dorval its base. Until they left for Trenton in 1959, the Squadron's North Stars carried troops to the Korean War, aid to refugees in Italy, flood relief to the Netherlands, re-supplied the DEW Line stations, and on 31 October 1951 brought Princess Elizabeth and Prince Philip to Dorval.

By 1947, Trans-Canada Airlines had given up its twelve-passenger Lancastrians for North Stars, built by Canadair at Cartierville a few miles away. They carried forty passengers and two tons (1,800 kilograms) of freight, and the effect this leap in payload capability had on Dorval's wartime terminal can be imagined. When North Stars were succeeded by Constellations that carried sixty-eight passengers, the old terminal was effectively outmoded. Additional land was expropriated to lengthen the runways and more buildings were erected. In 1955, the Department of Transport allowed American airlines to do their customs and immigration pre-clearance routine at Dorval.

On 19 March 1956, 426 Squadron's hangars burnt down, and North Stars and furniture were hurriedly pushed out into the snow on the ramp. The fire caused the RCAF to leave Dorval and reallocate at St. Hubert. Timmins

Dorval Airport adapting to commercial traffic in the late 1940s. During the war, this terminal building was the centre for Ferry Command and the Canadian Government Trans-Atlantic Air Service (CGTAS). (Air Canada Archives)

Aviation built the first cargo building near the old air terminal and in 1958, TCA decided to make Dorval the site of its new maintenance base for the Vickers Vanguards and later the DC-8s.

By 1956, the terminal that had been built for Ferry Command, and not the hundreds of civilian passengers that now flooded into it, was a ramshackle affair. At a cost of $30 million, work was begun on a new building in the wooded area to the east of the carpark. Dorval was also renamed Montreal International Airport (Dorval) and on 15 December 1960 the new air terminal was opened. Appropriately a plaque commemorating the airport's wartime role in the Atlantic Ferry was placed in the passenger lounge. By now, the airport that had been built as a wartime measure was processing two million passengers annually and competing with Malton to be the busiest in Canada.

An underground hydrant refuelling system was installed; the main runway 06L/24R was extended to 10,890 feet (3,300 metres); and in 1967, in time for the World's Fair, the transborder extension or finger was completed. A year later, a general aviation zone was laid out on the far eastern edge of the airport, with Execaire Aviation building a hangar and office on the site for its corporate aircraft.

The first Boeing 747 to land at Dorval in 1970 was Air Canada's and thousands of Montrealers came to Dorval Airport to walk through it.

As with all major airports, the use of wide-body jets by the airlines forced Dorval to build more runways, gates and ramps. The number of gates doubled when an aeroquay was built on the apron itself and connected to the terminal by tunnels. Yet by 1975, although eight million passengers were using the airport annually and the terminal was becoming dangerously overcrowded, Dorval was no longer the busiest airport in Canada, having been eclipsed by Toronto's Pearson.

The opening of Mirabel Airport north of Montreal, on 4 October 1975, relieved some of this congestion when all the international airlines transferred over and Dorval became purely for domestic and trans-border flights to the United States.

In 1983, Transport Canada began a revitalisation of the Dorval terminal, car parks and office buildings. The $34 million project, spread over three years, included a multi-level car park, airside facilities and the regional headquarters for Transport Canada. Canadair, now part of the Bombardier Group, built a major assembly plant between two runways at the northeast side of the airport for the manufacture of its Challenger jets.

As Dorval celebrated its fiftieth anniversary in 1991, its new control tower and fire station were being completed and Air Canada was building a training complex nearby. Because it, and not Mirabel, is the airport for trans-border traffic, Dorval is crucially affected by the Open Skies Treaty. Dorval had planned to put in a centralised U.S. Customs facility at a cost of $25 million. Now it is even more vital, said Paul Benoit of Aeroports de Montréal as within 1995-6, Dorval was to get 1.4 million additional "seats" — a forty per cent increase. The recent expansion of air side facilities like runways and tarmacs would help, but an investment in more loading bridges and gates was necessary.

Mirabel

Mirabel is an example of what happens to an airport when its fortunes are tied too closely to those of the city it was built to serve. Its present deserted state reflects that of Montreal's economy, as both stagger towards the next century with shattered dreams of what might have been. It wasn't always like this.

Having learnt from the problems associated with Toronto's International Airport in the mid 1960s, Transport Canada resolved to take the noise and environmental hazards that are part of an airport as far away as possible from the city it was to serve. In the euphoria of post-Expo '67, the federal government began planning for a second Montreal airport. Besides relieving the crowding at Dorval, it was to serve a grander purpose: as the trans-Atlantic air transport hub for Canada well into the twenty-first century. The parallels of making another Montreal airport the terminus for imperial dirigibles forty years before were obvious. This airport was going to be the exclusive point of entry for all trans-Atlantic flights to Canada and would be linked with Montreal and Toronto by a high-speed train. It was hyped as a showcase of our nation's future.

A site was chosen in 1969 near the village of St. Scholastique, northwest of Montreal near the Laurentians. There had been a farm and a railway station in the area called Mirabel, and this was taken as the new airport's name. The project was badly begun. Although the airport needed only 5,000 acres (2,000 hectares) of land, Ottawa expropriated 90,000 acres (36,000 hectares), opening itself to long, bitter legal battles with local farmers, some of whom eventually won back their farms. Construction started in June 1970 by BANAIM, the New Montreal International Airport Project Office, and 5,000 construction workers took to hacking out runways before the Laurentien foothills. The original estimate for the whole project was $500 million, but by the time Mirabel opened this figure had risen to $ 4 billion. For this price tag, five years later there were two runways (11-29 and 06-24), each 12,000 by 200 feet (3,658 by 61 metres), an air terminal with remote gates, a free standing control tower, an air cargo centre and a 361-room hotel. Unique to Canadian airports, aircraft were to be parked in servicing clusters and the passengers were transported to the terminal by PTVs (passenger transfer vehicles).

When, on 4 October, 1975, Prime Minister Pierre Trudeau officially opened Mirabel Airport, he called it the "harbinger of the year 2000." Twenty years later, when the airport celebrated its anniversary, amidst a bitter provincial referendum, his words must have seemed oddly prophetic. But at that time with Montreal hosting the Olympic Games the next year, it was an era for grandiose projects. Besides, the official Transport Canada prediction was that by 1990, there would be thirty million passengers using Mirabel and its future seemed assured.

By 1977, the effects of the OPEC oil crisis and the new 747s, with the range to overfly Montreal on the trans-Atlantic routes, were starving the airport of passengers. Four years after it opened, Mirabel saw barely 2.75 million passengers use it, while three times as many crowded through Dorval. The figure was worse in 1988 when Mirabel processed 2.5 million and Dorval 6.5 million. For unlike London's Gatwick Airport or Tokyo's Narita Airport, both of which are equally far away from the urban centres they serve, Mirabel had no rapid transit system to Montreal — let alone Toronto. The airlines forced to relocate to Mirabel from Dorval complained their customers preferred landing at an airport that was fifteen minutes to downtown, rather than taking an expensive bus ride from the foothills of the Laurentiens. To the businessman and tourist alike, even Toronto's Lester B. Pearson Airport, bursting at the seams, and far away Boston Airport were preferable. Not surprisingly several international airlines like Lufthansa, Alitalia and Canadian Airlines International have recently announced plans to drop their international services to Mirabel.[3]

By the late 1980s, Mirabel was infamous in the travel industry as Mizrabel, and by the less polite as The White Elephant. Indeed, the advertising agency hired to improve its image suggested cashing in on the nickname by using a white elephant as its logo. It was just that Montreal was too small to keep two airports in business. But given the huge investment in tax dollars and Dorval's popularity, it would be a brave government, federal or provincial, that even suggested closing down one of them.

3. Andre Picard, "Montreal Airport: 40 Years Ahead of its Time" *The Globe & Mail*, 10 October 1995, p.2.

Reviled by Canadian air travellers and tax payers, in 1994 Mirabel was ranked in an International Air Transportation Association survey as the fifth best airport in the world based on such criteria as: comfort, baggage handling, restaurants and shopping. (Canadair Archives)

Still, there were some positive signs. Thriving Canadair had outgrown its Cartierville site, and erected a hangar, buildings and a production plant at Mirabel for its military division. In 1987, the same year that Transport Canada built an apron and access roads for an aircraft maintenance area, Technair Ltd. erected its own hangar and administration building. From 1980 to 1987, Mirabel hosted an annual aviation fair, Expo Air, which saw aerobatic teams, United States Air Force C-5 Galaxies and thousands of spectators.

Possibly the best news for Aeroports de Montréal, the agency that took over both Dorval and Mirabel when Transport Canada privatized them in 1992, was that Mirabel contributed to half of the $25 million profits for 1994. While this is a fraction of what Vancouver, Calgary and Toronto made, in Montreal's depressed economy it is nonetheless welcome. But the very best news is that in a 1994 survey conducted by the International Air Transportation Association (IATA), travellers ranked Mirabel the fifth best airport in the world (after Amsterdam, Orlando, Singapore and Munich) on such criteria as comfort, baggage handling, connections, restaurants and shopping.

On February 20, 1996, Aeroports de Montréal announced that it is planning to transfer all scheduled flights from Mirabel to Dorval, and that Mirabel would take over all charter and cargo traffic for Montreal. In order to give Dorval Airport time to build added facilties to handle this influx, the move is scheduled to take place in April 1997.

Economists predict that when Dorval finally succumbs to urban development, Mirabel will come into its own. This is expected to occur around 2020 at the earliest. Thus Mirabel really is the showcase to Canada's future — even if that future has been slightly delayed.

Airports of the Northwest

In 1939 Canada, as part of the British Empire, entered World War II and focused on aiding Britain with pilots and aircraft. To protect the shipment of both these items across the Atlantic, airports were built in the Maritimes for anti-submarine patrols. Hundreds more were also constructed across Canada to provide training facilities for the British Commonwealth Air Training Plan (BCATP). However, the northwest of the country was remote from the European conflict and there was little urgency to improve the few airports already in place.

Grant McConachie, the owner of United Air Transport, had carved airfields out of the bush at Fort St. John, Fort Nelson and Watson Lake. Now with his pilots and aircraft being requisitioned for the war effort, McConachie must not have been alone in thinking that the development of the northwest was to suffer because of the European war.

This changed overnight on 7 December 1941, with the Japanese attack on the American naval base at Pearl Har-

bour, Hawaii and their subsequent invasion of the Aleutian Islands. Fear of losing access to the Pacific Ocean prompted the United States and Canadian governments to plan on reinforcing the west coast and Alaska by road and air. The Alaska Canada Military Highway, or ALCAN, was constructed by US troops and equipment. It opened on 20 November, 1942. Suddenly, airfields in the north that had known only the occasional bushpilot became vital to North American defence. Besides being used to defend Alaska, they had become part of the Northwest Staging Route. In 1942, as part of its lend–lease program to the Allies, the United States began ferrying aircraft to the Soviet Union through Canada and Alaska. Squadrons of fighters and bombers were assembled at Great Falls, Montana and flown to Alaska through the airports of Edmonton, Grande Prairie, Fort St. John, Fort Nelson, Watson Lake, and Whitehorse. At Fairbanks, Alaska, they were handed over to Soviet pilots. By the time the lend-lease

The Northwest Staging Route, the ALCAN Highway, and the CANOL (Canadian Oil) project caused the US and Canada to build a chain of airfields through northwest Canada to Alaska during the Second World War. (Air North Archives)

program terminated in 1945, over 8,000 aircraft had been ferried in this way and Canada's northwest gained a chain of fully operational airports, ports and roads.

Some airfields were also built for another wartime emergency. In 1941, fear of a Japanese attack on Alaska prompted the United States and Canada to find an alternative to their overseas oil supplies, then in danger of enemy submarines. To safeguard a wholly North American oil supply, a four-inch (10-centimetre) diameter pipeline was constructed from the Norman Wells oil field on the Mackenzie River, through the Richardson Mountains to Whitehorse, Northwest Territories. There a refinery was to be built to distribute the gasoline to Alaska and the Yukon. Called the CANOL Project (an acronym for Canadian Oil), this was a joint venture between Washington and Ottawa. As the pipeline could be completed only during the short summers, all goods and equipment had be freighted north by aircraft. Within twenty months, 52,000 workers completed the huge project, sometimes working at minus fifty degrees Centigrade. By this time the threat to Alaska had receded and the need for the pipeline did not exist. But as a byproduct of this, airfields were constructed or expanded at Fort McMurray, Hay River, Fort Simpson and Yellowknife.

Watson Lake Airport

By 1937, McConachie's Yukon Southern Air Transport (YSAT) was flying Barkley-Grow floatplanes to Lower Post, sixteen miles below Watson Lake. A year later, the company decided to abandon Lower Post and move their base up to Watson Lake. Log cabins were built for the staff and a radio/weather station for meteorological reports.

With the arrival of Lockheed Lodestars and DC-2s, the operation of floatplanes was becoming uneconomical and McConachie decided to switch to wheeled aircraft and build airports for them. YSAT engineers were clearing a landing strip at Watson Lake when world events caught up with them in the form of a government survey team. Even before the Pacific war began, Ottawa and Washington both felt some sort of air route in the northwest should be built in case of war. But it was not until Pearl Harbour, when Watson Lake became part of the Northwest Staging Route, that a second, larger airfield was constructed. The military engineers chose a site nine miles (15 kilometres) outside the town to put down a runway of 5,531 feet (1,676 meters) in length. The terrain was heavily forested and there were deep depressions caused by several creeks that ran through

it to the lake. Although it required extensive filling and levelling, the site was still the most suitable in the area.

Bringing men and equipment to Watson Lake to build an airport was a formidable task. All goods were first driven to Fort Nelson by truck, then barged to Wrangell. There, they were loaded onto small boats that took them up the Stikine River to Telegraph Creek on the old Klondike gold rush route. Once they got to Lower Post, they were trucked through to Watson Lake.

No sooner had the airport been laid out, than P-39 and P-40 fighters being ferried to the Russians began landing and taking off, with a precision that belied the inexperience of their ferry pilots. Soon an American unit was stationed at Watson Lake to aid in the ferrying operation. Overnight, this ballooned into a fully equipped US air base. With the war's end, the Americans departed, leaving behind a self-contained city at the airport with barracks, a theatre, a skating and curling rink and sportsfields.

McConachie's YSAT had become Canadian Pacific Airlines, which started scheduled services into Watson Lake in 1946. It took a decade for the Department of Transport to develop the site. The old US Army barracks were demolished; the lakeshore radio beacon was commissioned and private family dwellings erected.

Canadian Pacific began its 737 jet service to Watson Lake in 1968 and a maintenance garage and firehall were built the following year. Passenger and freight facilities were expanded through the 1970s and a VOR/DME air navigation system installed in 1975. An overnight campsite was laid out for pilots who wished to camp by the airport.

By the 1990s, the search for minerals in the area declined and with it the air traffic. All housing was removed from the airport to the town and the Flight Service Station decommissioned in 1991. The air terminal building is of 1942 vintage and the largest scheduled aircraft using Watson Lake is now a Beech 1900. As it is an Arctic Airport, federal subsidies will continue, but at a lower level and the property made available for transfer to the territorial government.

Cambridge Bay Airport

Cambridge Bay is 200 miles (322 kilometres) north of the Arctic Circle, on the south shore of Victoria Island. It has a nine month winter and, being above the treeline, is open to fierce blizzards. The only alternative to the airport is the short shipping season when material, fuel and vehicles can be brought into the harbour.

One of the first Europeans to visit Cambridge Bay was Roald Amundsen in 1905 as he navigated the Northwest Passage. He sold his ship, *The Maud*, to the Hudson Bay Company in 1927. It was used as a supply vessel and company warehouse in the harbour, eventually becoming the North's first radio station for weather reports.

In 1929, the first aircraft landed at Cambridge Bay but not at the site of the present airport. Cambridge Bay Airport is two miles (3 kilometres) from the town, and was surveyed late in the Second World War. Immediately after the conflict, both the USAF and the RCAF experimented with a world-wide navigation system called Beetle. It was decided to locate the radio transmitter and tower at Cambridge Bay Airport. When this navigation system became outmoded, the airport was given over to the Department of Transport and there seemed to be little future for it.

It was the construction of the Distant Early Warning (DEW) Line in the 1950s that made Cambridge Bay airport

A veteran of the frontier, this DC-3 at Dawson City airport represents the hundreds of her type that were used on construction of the DEW Line. (Air North Archives)

an important centre of transportation in the region. A terminal building was constructed and scheduled passenger service from the south was provided by Canadian North, First Air and Northwest Territorial.

The single runway is 5,033 by 152 feet (1,525 by 46 metres) and is surfaced by clay over crushed gravel. In 1992, 10,800 passengers and 5,545 aircraft had passed through Cambridge Bay. Like Watson Lake, Cambridge Bay is an Arctic Airport and federal subsidies will continue at a lower rate. With Fort Simpson, Iqaluit, Inuvik, Hay River and Resolute Bay, Cambridge Bay Airport will be made available for transfer to the territorial government.

Ottawa

Macdonald-Cartier International Airport

On July 19, 1919, a Curtiss JN-4 landed on the property of the Ottawa Hunt and Golf Club. In the absence of established airports, golf courses and polo grounds were considered acceptable landing fields and often the pilot or owner of the aircraft was a member of the club. The aircraft was being ferried from Toronto to Ottawa for its owners, E.J. Draper and W.M. Deisher of Reo Ottawa Sales Ltd. The club was conveniently situated on the southwest side of the capital, towards Toronto, for landing the Jenny.

This was not the first flight to take place in the Nation's Capital. On 11 September 1911, Len Hammond flew a biplane from Montreal over the crowds at the Central Canada Exhibition. He had planned to land at the Ex grounds but, with the spectators surging over the fairgrounds, gave up. As a result, Hammond used the cow pasture at Slattery's Field (now between Main Street and Echo Drive) for landing and taking-off. [1]

Neither the cow pasture nor the Hunt and Golf Club were envisaged as permanent aircraft landing facilities. In fact, the government and the public looked to an area east of the city where the new mode of transport might be used. Overlooked by the wealthy suburb of Rockcliffe, lay The Butts, a rifle range on the shore of the Ottawa River. A government-owned Curtiss Jenny carrying mail from Leaside, Toronto had already landed there in August, 1918 and several citizens, including the future Prime Minister William Lyon Mackenzie King, had motored out to see it. As the property was already owned by the government, on 19 April 1920, the Air Board established an aerodrome at Rockcliffe for military and civilian flying. At a time when there were as many seaplanes as land ones, the Rockcliffe facility had the added attraction of being on the riverbank and able to service both types of aircraft.

---

1. The local branch of the Canadian Aviation Historical Society has commerated the event by erecting a plaque at 35 Riverdale Avenue.)

The experimental airmail service between Ottawa and Toronto, 27 August, 1918. The future Prime Minister William Lyon Mackenzie King is third from the right. (National Archives of Canada PA 61493)

On the other side of the city, the Hunt and Golf Club sold off part of its golf course to Uplands Realty Co. and the airfield became known as Uplands. The field had a level surface and was unobstructed by trees in all directions. There were two grass runways, each 150 feet (46 metres) wide, approximately 600 yards (549 metres) in length. At their intersection was a hundred foot (30 metre) white circle. A windsock in the field's corner completed the airport.

The first international flight to land at Uplands took place on 15 April, 1920 when Lieutenant-Colonel H.E. Hartney and Captain H.T. Douglas, of the US Army, flew from Washington to Ottawa in a de Havilland DH-4. They refuelled several times along the way (the DH-4 had a range of 150 miles or 242 kilometres) and stopped overnight at Ithaca, NY. The United States Post Office was expanding its airmail routes and the DH-4 flight to Ottawa was considered a good test. In hope that the flight's publicity might attract some clients to use Uplands airport, on 14 May the Air Board proposed that a war-surplus hangar be put up and an aerial photography service begun, but the cost of both was prohibitive and the project was quietly dropped.

Then to celebrate Canada's Diamond Jubilee in July, 1927, American aviator Charles Lindbergh was invited to lead a formation of aircraft over the Parliament Building's new Peace Tower. Lindbergh had just completed his New York–Paris flight on 21 May and was, at that moment, the most famous pilot in history. He flew in from Mount Clemens, Michigan on 2 July and landed at Uplands, rather than at Rockcliffe. Most of the population of Ottawa came out to greet Lucky Lindy, causing a huge traffic jam along the country road to the village of Manotick. Five hundred soldiers from the Governor General's Foot Guards and the Cameron Highlanders provided the pomp, and crowd control. The RCMP quickly upstaged both regiments by mounting a guard over the Ryan monoplane.

At 1:19 EDT, *The Spirit of St. Louis* appeared over Uplands escorted by twelve Curtiss P-1B Hawks of the U.S. Army Air Service. The crowds, who had been waiting since dawn, cheered and honked their car horns. While Lindbergh landed, the Hawks performed a manoeuvre called a Lufbery Circle over the airfield. Upon alighting at Uplands, the Lone Eagle commented that the field was very muddy and crude. At that moment, one of his escort pilots, Lieutenant Thad Johnston, collided with another in the Circle. Wingless, Johnson's aircraft crashed into the ground, killing him instantly.

In spite of this, the triumphant tour to the city centre continued. Such was the adulation of the crowd that came to greet him at the airport, that Uplands was named Lindbergh Field in his honour. That night Prime Minister Macenzie King wrote in his diary, "A more beautiful character I have never seen. He was like a young god who had appeared from the skies in human form . . . as noble a type of the highest manhood as I have ever seen."[2]

If it was to be developed, only the Department of National Defence had the funds to improve Lindbergh Field. But the military were loathe to see their few resources going to another airfield, when it was well satisfied with their base at Rockcliffe. Besides, it was thought the Uplands site was too far from the city to be commercially useful.

When the federal government initiated the Flying Club Scheme in 1927 and began providing financial assistance to maintain airfields, the Ottawa Flying Club took over Lindbergh Field. The Club leased the land from Uplands Realty Co. for $300 annually and, in the depths of the winter of 1928, its aircraft began landing and taking-off from the airfield. A small club house was built on the road to the village of Manotick that passed by the runway. An airport license was obtained on 26 July, 1928, and the name Lindbergh Field was dropped and the original Uplands Aerodrome reinstated.

By 1935, in spite of the Depression, Uplands airfield boasted three hangars, an office and a windsock. This was insufficient evidence of progress for the Civil Aviation Branch of DND, which recommended the airport's license be suspended. The reason given was that no improvements had been made to the "rough surface" of the field. The inspectors advised that two 5,000 feet (1,524 metre) landing strips be laid and a total of $3,000 be spent on improvements.

The Club did not have the capital to finance the mandatory improvements and was forced to sell the lease to Laurentian Air Services. On 1 May, 1937, Laurentian leased the site from the Ottawa Flying Club for ten years at $720 a year. The company promised to allow the club use of the airport and to make all the improvements that the government wanted.

Laurentian went to the Department of Transport, and later the City of Ottawa, for financial assistance. The city declined but the federal government, after much lobbying, agreed to help. Uplands became a pet project for the new aviation-minded Minister of Transport, C.D. Howe, who took a personal interest in it. The airport was well-placed to become part of the Trans-Canada Airway, as it was a little north of the busy Montreal-Toronto air route and directly between the Maritimes and the western provinces.

2. Peter Robertson, "Young God From The Skies: Lindbergh at Ottawa, 1927" *CAHS Journal*, Winter 1987

Before the government could act, Laurentian shrewdly bought all 300 acres (120 hectares) of the airport outright from the Uplands Syndicate (formerly the Uplands Realty Co.) for $25,000. In what today would have led to a feeding frenzy by investigative reporters, the Department of Transport agreed to purchase the same 300 acres of the airport from Laurentian for $37,500. It also allowed the air company to lease the land its buildings were on for a dollar a year for twenty years and to keep the right to take-off and land without charge. It is no wonder that the company continues to operate from the airport today.

Construction began on improvements to the airport on 17 May 1938. It opened on 20 August 1938 with two runways: east–west 3,300 feet by 200 feet (1,006 by 61 metres) and north–south 3,000 feet by 200 feet (915 by 61 metres). Because it was designed to service the Trans-Canada Airway, lighting for night-flying, the latest in radio equipment and a meteorological office were installed. Part of the original Hunt Club clubhouse was leased for the radio technicians to live in. Mrs. Howe, the wife of Minister of Transport, officiated at the runway opening on 1 April, 1939, and the airport's name was changed (for the fourth time) to Ottawa (Uplands) Airport.

Trans-Canada Airlines (TCA) began operations into Uplands with their Lockheed Electras six months before the war in Europe broke out. Although Ottawa airport continued to be the local civil airport under the Department of National Defence, it became part of the British Commonwealth Air Training Plan's (BCATP) network of flying schools. On 2 August 1940, the Governor-General opened the RCAF base that housed No. 2 Service Flying Training School (SFTS). Four runways were paved and additional land was acquired along Bowesville Road for the sprawling airforce barracks.

Ottawa's airport even featured in a wartime Hollywood movie, *Captains of the Clouds*. It had occurred to the military that the public, in Canada and the United States, still didn't grasp why thousands of men and resources were being used for flying schools when they could be better put to immediate use fighting the Germans. A Hollywood movie to romanticise the yellow training aircraft, and the young men who learnt to fly them, seemed a brilliant idea. Canadian actor Raymond Massey, then under contract to Warner Brothers, heard of the plan and soon the studio had a script ready and assigned actor Jimmy Cagney to the starring role. Shooting started at Uplands in the summer of 1941, with the stars of the movie commuting from the Chateau Laurier and the camera men enduring the spartan Sergeant's Mess at the airport. A wet Ottawa summer hindered filming, as did the appearance of local VIPs, like the Governor General, the Earl of Athlone, who as a movie buff managed to appear on an inspection tour of the BCATP facilities at inopportune moments. *Captains of the Clouds* was a box office success,[3] its debut only upstaged by the news that the Japanese had bombed Pearl Harbour. However, from a historical point of view, it served to immortalize wartime Uplands — and the BCATP.

With aircraft production booming during the war, Uplands gained an industrial infrastructure as the Ottawa Car & Aircraft Ltd. set up their own factory for the manufacture and assembly of aircraft. Unfortunately, this was short-lived as the factory burned down in early 1944.

At the war's end, hangar space suddenly became a premium at the Airport. Trans-Canada Airlines stepped up its operations, and Canadian Colonial Airlines started to service Ottawa on its Montreal–Ottawa–Syracuse–Washington route. Because this was an international flight, Customs and Excise officers were accommodated at the airport, and Laurentian Air Services agreed to lease part of its hangar to them. Colonial put up a small cabin next to this hangar for the convenience of its own passengers.

In March 1947, the flying training school closed down and the RCAF moved out of the airport completely, making

Jimmy Cagney, star of *Captains of the Clouds* talks to Air Vice Marshall Billy Bishop, who also had a part in the film. (National Archives PL-5065)

---

3. Its director, Michael Curtiz, on the strength of *Captains of the Clouds*, was asked to direct *Casablanca* the following year, for which he won an Oscar.

four hangars and seven buildings vacant. The Ottawa Flying Club was given one of the buildings and half of a hangar on the Bowesville Road. The other half was occupied by Canadian Colonial Airlines and the Customs office. Trans-Canada Airlines declined to join them, preferring to remain at its terminal building on the north side of the airport.

The beginning of the Cold War forced the RCAF, in the form of Air Defence Command, to return to Ottawa airport. New hangars were built to house the Central Experimental and Proving Establishment and the headquarters of Air Material Command. It was envisaged that high speed jet fighters, like the Avro Arrow, would eventually be tested on the runways, and land was expropriated for future extensions of up to 25,000 feet (7,620 metres).

The Department of Transport also made it clear to the Ottawa Flying Club that it had to move its operations to Carp Airport, away from what was becoming an increasingly busy military and airline scene. The Club held out by replying that it would consider moving to Rockcliffe but not Carp. As one of the founders of Uplands Airport, the club members felt that they were being unfairly treated. A rumour made the rounds of Ottawa that when the RCAF Chief of Air Staff heard that a flying club was going to use Rockcliffe for a lot of frivolous recreational activities, he quickly telephoned the DOT to inform them the Air Force

could never condone such a move. The plan was quietly dropped and the Ottawa Flying Club continues today to operate out of its original site.

By now, the government had other problems: the demise of the Avro Arrow program in 1958 meant that the Proving Establishment had no revolutionary jet fighters to test, and its budget was slashed. Thus Uplands' runways were only extended to 10,000 feet (3,048 metres).

By 1954, the old terminal was becoming increasingly congested, as the North Stars and Constellations that the airlines now used carried twice as many passengers as the old Lockheeds. A temporary annex that included a snack bar and a Tilden Car rental office was built, while the DOT planned its $6 million terminal building, all glass and metal girders, to be completed by July 1959.

The new facility had a control tower, the airlines, the meteorological and Customs offices and a DOT school for air traffic controllers all under one roof. There was even space for the homeless National Aviation Museum, with its smaller artifacts located on the second floor, while at ground level, three historic aircraft were displayed. Unfortunately, just before the airport was to be formally opened in the summer of 1959, an American jet fighter saluted the new building by breaking the sound barrier over it. The force of the blast blew out the glass wall in the front of the

Ottawa airport's wedge-shaped terminal building displays none of the gloomy corridors or congested lounges of larger airports. (Ottawa Airport Authority photo)

terminal out and ripped the metal flashings off the roof along with most of the window panes. It cost $300,000 to repair the destruction. Not until June 30, the following year, could Prime Minister John Diefenbaker officially open the new terminal.

The airport underwent a fourth name change in 1964 when it became MacDonald–Cartier Airport. The terminal building was expanded and renovated in 1982 and again in 1987. Because it served the Capital Region, the Canadian Armed Forces was heavily involved in the airport. Their hangars were used for VIP welcoming ceremonies and military transportation flights and DND also provided the firehall and crash services.

The decade of the 1990s became one of great change for Macdonald–Cartier Airport. The management was forced to adapt to the downsizing of the military base at the airport. On the plus side, on 16 January 1995, Doug Young, the Minister of Transport Canada and David Gavsie, Chairman of the Airport Authority, signed a letter of intent to transfer the airport to a Canadian Airport Authority. At the signing ceremony, Mr. Gavsie said that he hoped that this would integrate the airport into the economy of the National Capital Region.

As if to complement this, on 24 February the Transport Minister and the United States Secretary of Transport signed the Open Skies air transport agreement. Any American air carrier who had for some time wanted to land at Ottawa, could now do so. US Air, Northwest Airlines and Delta (through its Business Express Connector) were quick to seize on this, connecting the capital with Pittsburgh, Chicago and Detroit. A major priority for Ottawa Airport would seem to be more air bridges and U.S. Customs pre-clearance booths.

The airy wedge-shaped terminal building displays none of the long, gloomy corridors, or congested lounges, of busier airports and is presently serviced by ten air carriers that range in size from Bearskin Airlines to KLM Royal Dutch Airlines.

Quebec City

Flying came to Quebec City in the person of George Mestach, an aviator from France who brought his Bleriot to the city's annual exhibition in 1911. On 30 August, Mestach took-off and circled around the fair. His speciality was an early form of airmail: he would carry messages to VIPs at the exhibition and drop them over the grounds. Mestach was a typical barnstormer who would later survive crashes in Winnipeg and Chicago before retiring from aviation.

In the 1920s, Quebec City's problem was that it lay between Rimouski and St. Hubert, the airport of Montreal. The federal government had built airports in both these locations for its airmail routes and, as a result, there was little incentive to invest in a third airport in the same province. Thus, the first airport for Quebec City was a private venture at St. Louis, in the western suburb of St. Foy. Today it is a park dedicated to pioneer pilot Romeo Vachon, and a plaque commemorates the site of the original airfield that he used.

Canadian Transcontinental Airways (CTA) bought the land at St. Louis in 1927 for an airport and built hangars and laid runways. Vachon and Clarence Alvin (Duke) Schiller, another aviation pioneer, began flying Fairchilds for CTA from St. Louis in 1928, when the federal government awarded CTA the contract to fly the winter airmail service between Rimouski and St. Hubert. When Canadian Airways bought up the company and the airport in 1931, it made Rimouski its base for the airmail run and moved out of St. Louis completely. Vachon, now District Superintendent of Canadian Airways, advised city officials that St. Louis would soon be abandoned as it was in danger of becoming part of suburbia. He recommended that another site further from the city limits should be selected as a municipal airport.

The fields of Ancienne Lorette, above sea level and ten miles (16 kilometres) outside the city, were ideal but the farmers who owned them wanted too high a price. It would not be until the Second World War that the Department of

Romeo Vachon (standing third from left) with a Curtiss JN-4. Quebec City's problem was that it lay between the government airports of Rimouski and St. Hubert, and there was little incentive to build a third airport in the same province. (National Archives of Canada C-61658)

Transport had the legal authority to take over the site for a flying school as part of the British Commonwealth Air Training Plan (BCATP). In 1940, the foundations for the first runways were laid, and a year later the City of Quebec Elementary Flying Training School set up and ran an air observer and flying training school at the airport. Ancienne Lorette soon had paved runways for the BCATP Ansons to take off and land on. Because teaching student pilots the rudimentaries of flying while there was a war taking place was disheartening and boring, the staff pilots did their best to enliven their flights.

"Favourite stunts were putting the Anson in a vertical dive and flying between the twin steeples of the Ancienne Lorette village church, flying under the Quebec City Bridge, making a low pass beside a ship on the St. Lawrence below the level of the main deck, and flying over Montreal at night low enough to look up at the illuminated cross on Mount Royal," wrote author Spencer Dunsmore.[1]

By 1943, Quebec Airways, a Canadian Pacific Air Lines subsidiary, began services from the airport to Montreal, Sept-Iles and Mount Joli. After the war, the BCATP establishment closed, leaving Quebec Airways as the only user of the airport. In 1946, the municipal authorities did not want to get involved with running an airport, and the Department of Transport kept the site and extended the runways.

In 1972, a new air terminal building was opened and renovated in 1984. Also used by a flying school and charter operations, Quebec/Jean Lesage International Airport is served by twenty-three scheduled passenger carriers and runs at a slight monetary surplus.

1. Spencer Dunmore. *Wings for Victory: The Remarkable Story of the British Commonwealth Air Training Plan in Canada.* McClelland & Stewart 1994, p.185

Regina

Aviation came to Regina immediately after World War I. On 19 May 1919, Lieutenant Roland J. Groome[1] in a Curtiss JN-4, landed outside Regina from Saskatoon. A week later, in what were the first cross country flights in the province, he took-off and flew to Moose Jaw. The privately owned airfield he used was on the corner of Hill Avenue and Cameron Street. Groome returned to Regina that year and, in partnership with Edward Clarke, formed the Aerial Service Company. One of the company's JN-4s would have the distinction of becoming the first aircraft to be registered in Canada as G-CAAA.

In 1927 the Regina Flying Club began their own airfield on another 160-acre (64 hectare) site outside the city, and they hired Groome as an instructor. When the National Flying Club movement began, Ottawa realized it could not build airports for every community across Canada that wanted one. Briefly, the federal government agreed to provide financial incentives towards the formation of a flying club. The City Councillors of Regina bought the Club's airfield in 1928 to take advantage of the scheme.

The development of the Prairie Air Mail Service changed Regina Airfield drastically. To emulate the success of the American and European airmail routes, in 1927 the Dominion Government took responsibility for creating a national airmail service. Starting in the prairies (with its flat and open terrain being the easiest area for such a scheme), Ottawa began to build airports, radio beacons, runway lighting and radio and weather services in the cities of Winnipeg, Saskatoon and Regina.

In October 1928, using Fokker Super Universals, Punch Dickins and Paul Calder of Western Canada Airways began an experimental mail service across the Prairie provinces. With Regina as a terminal, two routes were flown: from Regina to Winnipeg, and another from Regina to Saskatoon. The mail gathered at Regina airport was sorted

---

1. Groome received Canadian Commercial Air Pilot's Licence No.1 — the first ever in Canada. One of Canada's pioneer pilots, Groome was killed in an aircraft crash in 1935 while instructing a novice.

Regina Airport in 1941 was served by both Trans-Canada and Canadian Pacific Airlines. The Lockheed Lodestars on the apron were the backbone of wartime airline fleets. (Saskatchewan Archives Board R-B9616-2)

and then put in aircraft and flown east to Winnipeg and north to Edmonton. That fall, unusual weather conditions hampered flying across the Prairies and several times WCA aircraft were forced down because of blizzards.

In 1929, Dan McLean was appointed to the Civil Aviation Branch of the DND and headquartered at Regina. McLean was responsible for the construction of airports for the Prairie Air Mail Service. Through his influence, Regina airport's runways were the first to be asphalted and have lighting installed, so the first night mail could be flown by Canadian Airways Ltd. in 1930, and the municipal airport officially opened.

Trans-Canada Airlines began flying their transcontinental service through Regina in 1938 and, a year later, the Department of Transport built a solid-looking, two storey administration building and control tower.

During the Second World War, Regina Airport was taken over by the federal government for the flying schools of the British Commonwealth Air Training Plan and the RCAF built new hangars and strengthened the runways.

At the war's end, Trans-Canada Airlines began their North Star flights into Regina and a new airport terminal was opened on 12 October, 1960. The City of Regina took the airport back from the DOT in 1955 and struggled to maintain it financially. It was returned to the DOT in 1972. A modern air terminal building was erected in 1989 and, by 1992, the airport was being used by 578,917 passengers annually. The airport was still running at a deficit, the authorities aware that by 31 March 2000 all federal financial assistance will be phased out.

Airports of Toronto

Most of the early airfields in Canada were in the suburbs of Toronto. In 1910, a farm in Weston, north of Jane Street and Trethewey Drive was host to a distinguished gathering of aviation pioneers. On 9 July, the pilots and aircraft who had taken part in the air meet at Lakeside in Montreal came together once more for a fly-in on the farm of J.W. Trethewey. As in Montreal, the main attraction was the presence of the French aviator Count Jacques De Lesseps, the second man to fly the English Channel and son of the builder of the Suez Canal. The field where the air meet took place would be named after De Lesseps and, as it was in use until 1940, has the distinction of being the first airport in Canada.

Five machines competed: again it was a duel between the monoplane Bleriots and the biplane Wrights. The Bleriots had been sent from Montreal by rail, and their wings were warped from being carried in an open flat railcar. On 12 July as John Stratton was taking off in one, a control wire snapped and the aircraft crashed into the pine trees at the edge of the farm. But the next day, De Lesseps used the second Bleriot to fly over Toronto: a first for the city, the sight causing traffic and thousands of people to stop and watch the first aircraft they had ever seen 2,000 feet (610 metres) above.[1]

Aircraft were a novelty then and it took the carnage of the First World War for their potential to be realised. In 1915, Curtiss Aeroplanes & Motors Co. of Hammondsport, New York began two flying schools in Toronto to train pilots for the Western Front. At that time, a Canadian wishing to join the Royal Flying Corps had to learn to fly at his own expense and then go overseas. As the United States was still neutral, the American aircraft designer Glenn Curtiss and his Canadian partner, J.A.D. McCurdy, tried, with little success, to convince the federal government in

---

1. Canada owes much to the famous French aviator: the first to fly over Montreal and Toronto. On 18 October 1927, while taking aerial photographs off Gaspé, de Lesseps crashed into the sea. He was buried in the local village and overlooking the cliffs is a monument dedicated to him, sculpted by Henri Herbert.

Ottawa to begin an indigenous air force. Their motives were less than patriotic as the Canadian air arm was to be staffed by pilots trained in Curtiss Flying Schools and fly Curtiss-built aircraft. Curtiss and McCurdy set up a factory on Strachan Avenue in Toronto to build JN-3 training aircraft and purchased property for two flying schools. One was at Hanlan's Point on Toronto Island and the second a former rifle range at Long Branch.

Long Branch rifle range was at the corner of Dixie and Lakeshore Roads and sufficiently far away from the nearest residential area. The Curtiss Company levelled the land and the school was managed by John McCurdy himself, when he wasn't in Ottawa or London lobbying for government contracts. Pupils destined for the Royal Flying Corps were given their basic training on Curtiss flying boats at Hanlan's Point, and then graduated to the JN-3 wheeled aircraft at Long Branch.

The need for hundreds of trained aircrew increased as the war dragged on, and in 1917, the Royal Flying Corps (RFC) established its own training facilities in Canada. The Curtiss Company lost its monopoly on pilot training, and both Hanlan's Point and Long Branch were closed in 1916 and 1917 respectively. The British government chose two sites for RFC airfields near Toronto: Armour Heights (where Wilson Avenue meets Avenue Road) and Leaside, north east of the city (Eglington Avenue and Laird Drive).

At its height, Leaside was the largest, busiest airfield in the Dominion, with nine hangars and barracks for the personnel of three squadrons. At a time when it was customary for Canadian pilots to be sent to train in Texas during the winter, Leaside was the first airfield to remain open, operating through the snow with the JN-4s equipped with skis. As the airfields of the British Commonwealth Air Training Plan were destined to do in a future war, both Leaside and Armour Heights churned out hundreds of pilots. However, the First World War drew to a close and Leaside was destined to become famous for other events as well. The first official airmail flight ended at the airfield on 24 June, 1918 when Captain Brian Peck of the RAF flew a sack of mail from Montreal to Toronto.[2] Later on 15 August and 4 September 1918, airmail flights were made from Leaside to Ottawa. The airport was also used by contenders in the New York–Toronto–New York air race of September 1919. In the 1920s, Ericson Aircraft Ltd., the Aero Club of Canada and the Toronto Flying Club all established themselves at the airfield. It was to become Toronto's municipal airport and in May 1928 Canadian Airways used it for their

---

2. A plaque at 970 Eglington Avenue East, erected by the Ontario Archaeological Board, commemorates the event.

Toronto–Montreal flights. When Leaside closed in 1931, the airlines and clubs moved to De Lesseps Field.

With the end of the First World War, trained pilots and war-surplus aircraft became readily available, and airfields, aero clubs and air charter concerns sprang up in the suburbs of Toronto. They were home to small companies like Toronto Airways, Manning Brothers, Bishop–Barker Aeroplanes Ltd. and National Air Transport. The aviators barnstormed, gave flying lessons, built hangars, lobbied for airmail routes from the government and caught the imagination of a restless public.

Several airfields sprouted around Toronto's northern suburbs, especially around the farms on Dufferin Street, north of the city. The larger were Willowdale (on Yonge and above Finch), Canadian Air Express Airport (bounded by Wilson, Dufferin and Shepherd Avenues), Newtonbrook (on the east corner of Yonge and Finch Avenues), Barker (on the corner of Lawrence and Dufferin) and Mount Dennis. Barker Field closed in 1953 and others were gradually amalgamated into Mount Dennis airfield (between Dufferin and Keele Streets). To be renamed Downsview Airport, Mount Dennis had been constructed in 1929 by the De Havilland Aircraft Co. Ltd. and was t

produced trainers and fighter-bombers and expanded the airfield to take over others in the surrounding area. In the postwar years, when Malton became too busy for RCAF operations, the Department of National Defence moved there as well.

Toronto Air Harbour and Island Airport

With the closure of the Curtiss Flying School in Toronto Harbour, it was not until 1921 that the next important aviation event took place. On 14 May, the flying boat *Santa Maria* landed in the harbour and taxied up to the Harbour Commission building. The building's roof was crowded with spectators to see the air cruiser on her historic journey from Havana, Cuba to Detroit. She had made the last hop from Belleville in an hour and forty minutes.

The *Toronto Telegram* reported the aircraft could accommodate eleven passengers and a crew of four. The reporter noted the two cabins on board were finished in mahogany and silver and there were upholstered chairs. It was hoped a regular s

crowds of appreciative Torontonians. The euphoria that characterized the 1920s was at its height then; when in the summer of 1929, the Royal York Hotel was officially opened, many members of the media flew in from New York for the ceremony. The hotel, one pilot said, was an excellent landmark for locating the Toronto waterfront. Anticipating renewed international attention on the waterfront, the Toronto Harbour Commission built a seaplane base at the edge of Scott Street, east of Yonge. Called an "air harbour" the facility had its own refuelling dock, crane and ramp and was designed to give passengers immediate access to downtown Toronto. Colonial Western Airways took advantage and inaugurated its Buffalo–Toronto flights on 15 June 1929 to carry mail between the two cities. Its Sikorsky S-38 amphibian waddled up the ramp to be christened *Neekah* (thought to mean goose) by Mrs. Howard Ferguson, wife of the Premier of Ontario.

The effects of the Depression curtailed any expansion in the international service and the publicity stunts. It would not be until 1937 that the crowds came out to Toronto harbour once more to watch another group of visitors land. Reflecting the uncertain times, these were British naval aircraft from two Royal Navy vessels visiting

still be a year before Toronto Island Airport opened, anchored near the Royal Canadian Yacht Club where the fliers were taken to lunch.

In 1931, the Toronto Harbour Commission sought to build a combined airport/air harbour on Toronto Island. At a time when sea and landplanes were developing with equal speed, it was difficult to predict where the future lay. There was great opposition to this from the community living on Toronto Island — a battle which continues to the present day. Although the island was prone to fog and only accessible by ferry, the Department of National Defence proposed the seaplane ramp be maintained at Scott Street and an airport be built on the Island. The fight between the harbour commissioners, the islanders and the Mayor of Toronto raged on through the 1930s, until the federal government stepped in and a compromise was reached.

In 1936, C.D. Howe, the federal Minister of Transport, offered to contribute to the cost of building airports in Toronto and all parties appeared mollified by this. Two airports would be built as alternates to each other in case of bad weather. The federal government would contribute $100,000 in 1937, $250,000 in 1938 and $100,000 in 1939. E.L. Cousins, general manager of the Toronto Harbour Commission, recommended the second airport be located

In 1940, the Norwegian government negotiated with the Toronto Harbour Commission to use the Toronto Island airport as a training base. The base's entrance was at the Lakeside Home's summer hospital, where this guard stands watch. (Royal Norwegian Embassy)

Toronto Harbour Commissioners formally agreed to build and operate both airports on behalf of the city.

Residents were given notice to vacate Hanlan's Point in December 1937, paying for their own removal in exchange for three years free rent from the city. That summer, 150 acres of the Point were sodded and two runways were laid out. A cable ferry was put in on the Keating Channel and a terminal building identical to the one at Malton[3] built. When King George VI paid a visit to Toronto in 1939, the city named the airport after him. But even then the idea of bestowing such a grand name on so sleepy an airport must have seemed ludicrous and it has never been used.

It took World War II to change sleepy Toronto Island airport dramatically. In June 1940, Norway was overrun by the Germans and the Norwegian government asked Canada if it could provide training facilities for the Norwegian Air Force. Ottawa was fully occupied in setting up the British Commonwealth Air Training Plan (BCATP) and all available aircraft and airfields had been allocated to it. But the Norwegians possessed substantial funds from their merchant fleet, and Scandinavian communities across North America generously donated aircraft. Accordingly, the Norwegian government successfully negotiated with the

---

3. It is today listed as a historic building, the only airport terminal to be so honoured.

Toronto Harbour Commission for the use of Island Airport as a training base.

Even before the hangars and barracks were ready, the Toronto Flying Club began training the Norwegians on their Tiger Moths. On 10 November 1940, the flying school on Toronto Island Airport was opened as "Little Norway." The aircraft chosen for elementary training were the Fairchild PT-19 or Cornells and later supplemented by the Douglas A-5 dive bombers, that had been ordered by the Norwegian Army before the German invasion. As it had in the previous world war, Hanlan's Point filled once more with pilots billeted in the Lakeside Home's summer hospital building.

The Norwegians loved flying over the Canadian lakes and forests because it reminded them of home. They also were, one pilot recalls, especially popular with the Canadian girls. "They all seemed to believe that we had swum the North Sea or crossed over the North Pole on skis," he said. "Even when I told them that I had just gone ashore from a ship in a Canadian harbour quite peacefully, the girls just winked knowingly and remarked that they knew I could not tell the real story because I feared reprisals to my family

Toronto Island Airport became "Little Norway" during the Second World War. Its terminal building, in the background, is still in use today. (Royal Norwegian Embassy)

In January 1941, Crown Price Olav of Norway and Crown Princess Martha inspected their airmen on the island. Because of the ice conditions at Toronto in the winter, training was transferred to Jericho Beach, Vancouver. In the summer, flying resumed at Toronto Island Airport. Then on 20 June, the worst fears of the Islanders were confirmed when a Norwegian aircraft collided with the Island ferry, killing both the student pilot and the instruc-

at Little Norway and more arrived each day. The decision was taken to move the school to a recreation camp near Gravenhurst in the Muskokas, north of Toronto. There an emergency landing strip was developed into a large and busy flying school, unofficially called "Lille Bergen."

Little Norway closed on 16 February 1945, but a small Norwegian Air Force unit remained at the Island Airport until 1947, packing and shipping the aircraft and equipment home. The barracks were used as emergency housing until torn down a decade later. On 18 September 1976, Crown Prince Harald of Norway dedicated a plaque at the Island Airport in memory of its days of wartime glory when it was known as Little Norway.

After the War, once more due to the availability of surplus airforce pilots and aircraft, recreational flying became popular and Island Airport, close to downtown Toronto, quickly filled with both. In 1961, the runway was enlarged to 4,023 feet (1,219 metres) and lighting installed for night flying. But as access to the Island was limited to a single ferry boat and the height of buildings on the Toronto waterfront grew every year, the airport has never reached its full potential and runs at an annual deficit of $1.7 million. With the development of De Havilland's Short Take Off and Landing (STOL) aircraft, it was hoped that the Island Airport would have a role as an alternate to Pearson. But throughout the years, the City Councillors vetoed this, only giving way in 1985 to allow the use of De Havilland Dash 8s on a limited passenger service. With a tunnel to replace the aging ferry and allowing the new generation of small jet airliners to land (most of which are quieter than the turbo-props currently being used), Island Airport will have a future. In August 1995, Toronto's Mayor Barbara Hall attempted some sort of compromise by asking for an environmental study of the building of a tunnel. Until its results are published, the businessmen and airlines that would use the airport, and thereby help wipe out its deficit, can only hold their breath.

Malton (Lester B. Pearson) Airport

At first few were in favour of an airport in the farmlands north of Toronto. The Toronto Flying Club even bought a large newspaper ad claiming: Malton was too far away; it would cost too much to build; and no one would drive there. P.C. Garrett, the managing director of De Havilland Aircraft stated he disliked the site. Keith Russell, I/C No. 10 Squadron RCAF told the press on 28 May 1937: "The Malton field is absolutely impossible as far as our men are concerned. We won't be able to get our men that far. It's about twenty-five miles from the east end of the city. I'm afraid for No. 10 if we have to go to Malton."

But C.D. Howe was committed to building an airport for Toronto and Malton offered room for expansion. That summer thirteen local farms, at a total of 1,050 acres (420 hectares), were bought at $100 an acre. Even as the land was being drained, R.J. Magot, a Toronto businessman, built the first of many aircraft manufacturing plants at Malton. The 60,000 square foot (5,400 square metres) National Steel Car Corporation bid for, and got, the contract to build the British–designed Westland Lysander.

By 1938, Malton had two hard-surfaced runways, a

In 1939, this terminal building, a replica of the one still at Toronto Island airport, replaced the farmhouse that had been purchased with the property. (L.B. Pearson International Airport Archives)

farmhouse, where the air traffic controllers could signal the aircraft. A bus service to Malton was inaugurated on 31 October with four daily trips and two on the weekends. As there were no airline passengers, the bus was used by workers at National Steel Car and the new Canadian Associated Aircraft Ltd. factory.

On 24 January, 1939 the Toronto Harbour Commission received a license to operate Malton Airport. A new

The first aircraft to land at Malton was this American Airlines DC-3 on 29 August, 1939. At the ceremony, the mayor of Toronto unsuccessfully tried to name the airport after Canada's greatest air ace, Billy Bishop. (L.B. Pearson International Airport Archives)

second floor. On 29 August, the first aircraft to land at Malton was an American Airlines DC-3. The airport was nominally under the control of the Harbour Commission and thus the City of Toronto, but was leased to the Department of Transport. The mayor of Toronto wanted the new airport to commemorate Canada's greatest air ace, Billy Bishop, but DOT policy insisted on identifying the airport by the region and the name remained Malton.

A Trans-Canada Airlines Lockheed flew the airline's first flight into Malton on 17 October 1938, connecting it with Montreal and Vancouver. The first air shipment consisted of orchids, men's suits, chewing gum and newspapers.

The first aircraft to be built at the National Steel Car factory at Malton was a Lysander II, which took to the air on 17 August 1939, just in time for the Second World War. Later Hampden bombers and Avro Ansons were also built at the plant. In 1942 the federal government took over the factory, renamed it Victory Aircraft Ltd., and began construction of the famous Lancaster bomber.

On 8 May 1940, Malton began a new air traffic control system: with men on duty twenty-four-hours a day to operate the landing beacons and smoke pots (which were used

and the No. 1 Air Observers School, both part of the British Commonwealth Air Training Plan. The Toronto Flying Club moved to the airport and as part of its war effort, formed the Malton Flying Training School.

The first Canadian-built Lancaster, *The Ruhr Express*, left Malton on 7 August 1943. Towards the end of the war, work was begun on its successor, the Lincoln. When the war ended, the federal government sold the facility to A.V. Roe Ltd. This forward-looking company began work on jet aircraft: fighters and airliners. These were heady days at Malton, as it became the site of the first North American jet airliner, the Avro C.102 Jetliner, and the first Canadian-built jet fighter, the CF-100. The Jetliner flew in 1949, five years ahead of Boeing's 707. Although it was successfully evaluated by no less a pilot than Howard Hughes himself, there was little commercial interest and Avro was reluctantly forced to abandon it.

Civilian air services continued during the war with American Airlines flights from Buffalo and TCA's service to New York with Lockheed Lodestars. TCA also built a hangar on the south corner of the apron. Catering for its flights was supplied by the Canada Railway News Co., from a restaurant at the railway terminal at Sunnyside. When the old farm house became vacant in 1941, the caterers

An aerial view of the airport in 1987, its bays already crowded. The aeroquay in the centre, radical for its day, was inadequate to meet the demands of the jumbo jet era. Terminal 3 was not yet built. (L.B. Pearson International Airport Archives)

provided by Carter Livery. Hertz Rent-A-Car opened an office in 1950 and the first of the vast car parks was laid out in 1951.

The Department of Transport upgraded Malton immediately after the war, installing an instrument landing system (ILS) in 1948 and extending runways 14-32 and 10-28.

More exciting was the development of the Avro Arrow at Malton. On 25 March, 1958, test pilot Jan Zurakowski took off from the airport in the first Arrow. In Canadian aviation history, the flight was comparable to J.A.D. McCurdy taking off from Baddeck, Nova Scotia. The Avro factory was busy and the apron outside its hangar was littered with CF-100 fighters and a couple of Arrows. The whine of the Canadian-made Iroquois engines fitted to the Arrow made Malton an exciting place to work. When Prime Minister John Diefenbaker cancelled the Arrow program on 20 February 1959, the company's personnel were devastated and production ceased. Avro never recovered and De Havilland of Canada took it over in 1962. That company itself was bought out by McDonnell Douglas in 1969.

By the late 1950s, the airport was a hodge-podge of buildings as it attempted to keep pace with the demands

Malton was British Overseas Airways Corporation (BOAC). By 1962, almost 1.5 million passengers had used Malton and for the first time it surpassed Montreal's Dorval Airport.

In 1958, the airport was completely redesigned with an aeroquay at the southeast corner of the airport. Its name was changed from Malton to Toronto International Airport (Malton). Radical for its day, the aeroquay was circular and expensive to build, but aircraft could park around it and passengers had less distance to walk. Cars approached the terminal through a tunnel under the apron and a parking garage was built in the centre. Even as the aeroquay was being constructed, an air cargo complex was built by WIG-MAR Investments to the north of the aeroquay. The aeroquay was opened by Prime Minister Lester B. Pearson on 28 February 1964. But two years later, so quickly had passenger traffic increased, it was already congested. TCA's successor, Air Canada, had over a hundred daily flights landing at Malton and several American airlines like Eastern, Mohawk, United and North Central were also eager to increase their traffic.

The noise of the early jets taking off and landing annoyed the residents of the suburbs that had crept up around Malton and there was vociferous pressure to prevent any

port began to look at sites as far from residential areas as possible, and Pickering was chosen. Here too, there was public opposition and plans for a second large Toronto airport at Pickering were dropped in 1975. Instead, the Department of Transport sought to develop Malton's terminals.

Terminal II was specifically designed with jumbo jets in mind, and even as construction began in 1969 over five million passengers were crowding through the aeroquay. In 1971, an omen of the age of wide-bodied jets landed at Malton: an Alitalia Boeing 747. That year, Air Canada began using 747s as well, and growth in traffic, both aircraft and passenger, was unprecedented. In desperation, the Department of Transport leased the air cargo building as a temporary terminal to process thousands of charter passengers. The following summer, these were moved to the incomplete Terminal II.

By the mid 1970s, the 747s of KLM, Swissair, Air France, and Lufthansa were all disgorging their passengers at Toronto International. Local feeder airlines, like Nordair and Air Ontario, added to the traffic problems. By late 1979, in spite of extensions to the terminal buildings and increased space for car parks, with fourteen million passengers Canada's major airport was barely coping. There were from sixty-eight air companies operating out of the airport.

Air Canada, CP Air and Wardair built new maintenance hangars for their 747 fleet. The chaos that threatened to engulf Toronto International Airport seemed inevitable.

The airport was forced to cope with other problems as well. Inured as we are, in this post-Lockerbie era, to the heavy security measures at modern airports, it is difficult to believe that scarcely two decades ago they did not exist at all. Before the security fences and guard booths were erected in the 1970s, a driver could park his car beside Highway 401 and walk onto the airport runway. Worse, Britannia Road, not far from the 401, was sometimes mistaken by motorists as a means of access to Terminal 1. The only security measure between it and the airport's runways was a sign that read "Authorised Traffic Only". It was only a matter of time before several drivers enroute to the terminal found themselves on Runway 14-32, and in one case sharing it with a DC-9 about to take-off.

If fences prevented errant motorists from the runways, they were useless against the other invaders — birds. The ingestion of a bird into a jet engine, especially during the critical stages of an aircraft's flight (landing or on take-off) can have deadly consequences for both parties. Like their colleagues at Vancouver Airport, Malton's employees had used fire crackers and bird distress calls to frighten the flocks off the runways. But besides being inconclusive, the program was expensive to maintain. When in 1973 the noted naturalist, Red Mason, asked to try his falcons, providing them free of charge, the Airport's management was ecstatic. Dramatically, bird strike statistics dipped to almost nil and the use of Mason's falcons spread to other airports. By 1980, a sophisticated bird mews was constructed at Pearson, housing up to fifteen raptors on any day. The bird control contractor would select the particular species of raptor for the type of bird on the runway. The demonstrations staged for visitors were especially popular with school parties.

In 1981, the Department of Transport unveiled a master plan to improve conditions by building a third terminal and expanding ground transportation. As aircraft were forced to park further away from the terminal, passenger transfer vehicles were bought from Edmonton Airport to ease the strain. On 1 January, 1984 Toronto International was renamed Lester B. Pearson Airport. Terminal II was extended and in 1986 a helicopter shuttle provided connector flights to downtown Toronto. However, when the residents of Etobicoke objected to the noise, it was discontinued.

In 1987, the federal government asked for bids from

and the contract was awarded to a joint venture between Lockheed Airline Terminal and Toronto-based developers Huang & Danczkay. The chosen architectural firm of Bregman and Hamann sought inspiration for the terminal's design in the railway stations of Victorian Europe. Less than three years after the contract was awarded, Terminal III, called Trillium, opened. The airy, curved expanse of white metal latticework had cost $560 million and its 133 acre (53 hectare) site alone could serve twelve million passengers. Trillium's two piers reached out, like welcoming arms, to as many as twenty-four docking aircraft simultaneously and the whole terminal was connected by an enclosed walkway, with its own 3,300-car garage and 500-room hotel. The entire length of the Grand Hall, that served as the check-in and ticketing area, was covered by a vaulted glass ceiling — reminiscent of the railways stations of nineteenth century London or Paris, but without the steam and soot. From the day it opened, Trillium was a positive monument to privatization.

"Everybody wins," said Viggo Butler, president of Lockheed Air Terminal. "The people of Toronto got their airport and the new revenues it generates, air travellers got improved service and we got a very profitable property."

The City of Toronto, which had kept the airport at

The architects who designed Terminal III, Trillium, sought inspiration for its vaulted glass ceiling from the great Victorian railway stations. (Bregman & Hamann Corp.)

surprised that the private sector could turn it into a cash cow. Pearson today accounts for more than 56,000 jobs, $1.9 billion in income and $630 million in tax revenue.

During the dying days of the federal Conservative government in 1993, the bill to privatise Pearson International was hastily finalised and became a political embarrassment to Prime Minister Kim Campbell. The opposition party severely criticised the privatisation bill, claiming that the contract had gone to the Pearson Development Corporation, a consortium of developers linked to the Conservative Party.

Once the Liberals came to power, they kept their election promise to cancel the privatisation contract and forbade the developers to go to court to seek compensation. The developers launched a lawsuit against the government to be reimbursed for the $445 million they had lost in the deal. The Conservative-dominated Senate and the Liberal government remained at an impasse while all improvements to the airport came to a standstill. Until the political fallout is resolved, the Lester B. Pearson International Airport Master Plan remains in limbo.

Vancouver

In British Columbia, Vancouver's Minoru Park Race Track on Lulu Island was the scene of several firsts in early aviation. On 25 March 1910, an American, Charles K. Hamilton, arrived from Seattle, Washington to give demonstration flights. He attracted an audience of 3,500 who watched him race against an automobile and later a horse. More importantly for aviation, on 28 March, Hamilton ventured out of the race track and flew a circuit to New Westminister. The first Canadians to fly in British Columbia also used Minoru Park. On 23 September 1911, the Templeton brothers, William and Winston, built and flew a tractor-biplane from the site. Finally, the park was used as an airfield by William Stark on 12 April 1912 when he flew at a height of 500 feet (155 metres) to the mouth of the Fraser River.[1]

Another early airfield was Hastings Park. But local aviators did not much care for it, as it was small with a high forest on three sides and a hydro-electric line on the fourth. Yet, from it on 24 May 1912, two daring Americans, Clifford Turpin and Phil Parmalee, managed to take off in a two seater biplane and fly over Burrard Inlet. On their way home disaster struck. The Canadian railway company refused to carry their aircraft, perhaps because they had a premonition about future competition, and the Americans had to persuade a taxi-driver to take the engine in his cab's back seat and put the wings on the roof.

In 1915, Stark opened a flying school at Minoru Park with an OX-powered Curtiss pusher aircraft. One of his pupils was Murton A. Seymour, who in 1939 was awarded the Trans-Canada Trophy in recognition for his work with the Flying Clubs of Canada. In 1915, Seymour graduated from Stark's school and organised the Aero Club of British Columbia, the first flying club in Canada. He set up the club at an airfield on Sea Island, exactly where the present Vancouver International Airport now stands.

1. Although the event was well covered by the local press, news of the Titanic disaster throughout it to the back pages.

Race tracks continued to serve as informal landing grounds for many years. On 7 August 1919, Captain Ernest Hoy took off from Minoru Park in a JN-4 for the first flight through the Rockies. On 17 October 1920, Flight Lieutenant G.A. Thompson landed at Brighthouse Park race track in a DH9A. He was the last participant in the historic first flight across Canada of the newly created Canadian Air Force (CAF). Begun on 7 October, the flight had taken place in stages with CAF seaplanes flying the Halifax–Winnipeg section and DH9A landplanes the Winnipeg–Vancouver part.

Jericho Beach

Immediately after the First World War, Vancouver had an air harbour nearby which, although run by the military, was engaged in purely civil duties. After the First World War, the role of the Air Board (as the Air Force was called) was anything but clear and the government used the organization in a number of civilian operations, from flying airmail routes to forestry patrols.

In 1919, the Air Board conducted a national survey of potential airfield sites where government aircraft could be based. On the Pacific coast, it selected Jericho Beach, near

were built. The first aircraft used at Jericho Beach was an H2SL flying boat for forestry and fishery patrols. In 1920, the aircraft was required to fly anti-smuggling patrols for Customs and chemical-spraying flights (to eradicate mosquitos) for the provincial government. Then larger Felixstowe F3s arrived as gifts from Britain. Ungainly and ill-suited to the diverse tasks they were made to perform, the Felixstowes were not a success. In 1922, the Air Board stations were closed across Canada and replaced by air force training units. Jericho Beach was made the principal Pacific coast air station through the 1920s and no longer involved in civil duties.

Sea Island

In 1928, the City of Vancouver leased a field on Lulu Island near Landsdowne Park for the Aero Club which was then still at Sea Island. It was understood this was a temporary solution for a permanent site for a municipal airport. Two runways, 2,706 feet (820 metres) and 1,268 feet (384 metres), a hangar and a passenger lounge were built on Lulu Island. Ford Trimotors belonging to British Columbia Airways used the airfield on their Vancouver–Victoria service.

The Aero Club preferred Sea Island and managed to convince the city that it was more suitable. It was totally available for expansion. The lobbying was successful. The city purchased 475 acres (190 hectares) on the island for an airport and hired pioneer aviator William Templeton as the first airport manager. Templeton would remain as manager until 1950, steering the airport through its lean and hungry years. Years later, he recalled moving the entire Lulu Island Airport staff, consisting of three men and a horse, with a wagon over to Sea Island. The horse, he would later say, provided more than transport as it kept the grass on the runways down as well. The municipal airport, called Sea Island Airport, was opened on 22 July, 1931 with one runway 2,416 feet (732 metres) in length, an office building and two hangars. After St. Hubert, Quebec it had the second terminal built in Canada.

Templeton realized that Ottawa, Toronto and Montreal were too far away for airline service, and that to make his airport more viable it would take active courting of air companies from below the border. In 1932, he convinced Alaska Washington Airways to begin a service from Seattle to Vancouver and in 1934 United Airlines inaugurated a Seattle–Vancouver route, using its new Boeing 247s. While this helped, the airport was still not financially viable and in 1935, the city of Vancouver offered it to the Department of National Defence as a military base. DND stated that it saw no reason why Vancouver should be given preferential treatment over other cities and declined. But it did donate a communications and meteorological office.

As the Pacific terminus for the Trans-Canada Airway, two runways were hard-surfaced to 914 metres (3,027 feet), lighting was provided for night flying and a taxiway added. On 29 July 1937, the famous trans-continental flight bearing C.D. Howe touched down at Vancouver Airport and The Trans-Canada Airway had become a reality.

Vancouver was also connected to the North by Yukon Southern Air Transport. The airline's Lockheed Lodestars flew from the airport to Prince George, Fort Nelson and Whitehorse. In September 1937, Trans-Canada Airlines (TCA) began its Vancouver–Seattle run and in March 1938, started an airmail service across the Rockies to Winnipeg. By 1 April 1938, passengers were able to fly between Montreal and Vancouver on TCA.

Although the Second World War was initially far away from Vancouver, the military took the airport over in 1939. This was what the city had for many years hoped for, as the federal government financed major airport improvements such as lengthening the runways and building more hangars. That year, Sea Island saw the arrival of the Blackburn Sharks of RCAF 6 Torpedo Bomber Squadron, with the Hawker Hurricanes of No. 1 (F) Squadron. The Hurricanes, at that time the most modern fighters Canada possessed,

were delivered to Sea Island in crates and assembled at the airport.

As part of the British Commonwealth Air Training Plan, an Elementary Flying Training School (EFTS) was opened at the airport and operated by Vancouver Air Training Co., the successors of the Aero Club of BC. In 1941, with America still neutral, a large Boeing aircraft-parts factory was built at the airport to take advantage of the huge orders for B-17 Flying Fortresses that England was expected to put in. The Seattle company was no stranger to Vancouver, having manufactured seaplanes at the Hoffar–Beeching Shipyards in 1929.

After the war, the airport was returned to the city and in 1948 renamed Vancouver International Airport. It was truly international as British Commonwealth Pacific Airways (later to become QANTAS) flew in from Sydney, Australia and on 10 July 1949, Canadian Pacific Airlines, the successor to Yukon Southern Air Transport, began flying North Stars to Hawaii, Australia, Tokyo and Hong Kong.

The airport became home to two people destined for fame in Canadian aviation history. In 1950, Carl Agar, the manager of Okanagan Air Service at Vancouver Airport, was awarded the Trans-Canada Trophy for his work in operating helicopters in mountainous terrain. Vancouver was also made the home base for Canadian Pacific Airlines and its president, the legendary Grant McConachie, who had developed it from a bush operation to an international airline.

As passenger traffic expanded through the 1950s and '60s, more terminal buildings were put up. The original 1930 building was destroyed by fire in 1949 and a temporary one erected on the north side. The Korean War increased air traffic towards the Far East as United Nations troops were airlifted through Vancouver to Tokyo. The North Stars of RCAF 426 Squadron bore the brunt of the airlift and took off from Vancouver Airport regularly with troops and supplies and returning with litters of wounded men.

On 30 December, 1953, as RCAF North Star 17503 took off from the Airport, its number four engine began to overheat and the pilot turned back. Visibility was marginal and heavy icing increased the aircraft's stall speed so it approached the runway too steeply. First the nose wheel and then the starboard wing ploughed into the ground. Then the wing broke off and the North Star flipped over on its back. In an amazing display, it slid upside down through a shower of sparks the length of the runway, finally coming to rest a few yards from the crash tenders. Even as gasoline began to spurt out of the aircraft's tanks, one

Well positioned as the North American gateway for the Asia-Pacific region, Vancouver International Airport has financed its expansion with unpopular "airport improvement fees". (Department of Transport photo)

fireman recalled seeing the passengers climb out unscathed, only to stand around the wreck and light up cigarettes.

On board the North Star had been the World War II RCAF air ace Robert W. (Buck) McNair. He immediately organized the rescue operations and later received the Queen's Commendation for Brave Conduct. The fact that none of the fifty-four passengers were hurt is a tribute to

In 1957, a west terminal was opened at Vancouver Airport to take the strain off the old one. With over 700,000 people using the airport annually, the north terminal was renovated and kept in service. By now the airport was becoming too expensive for the city to operate and in 1962, Vancouver sold its investment in the airport to the Department of Transport. This paid off as the federal government began funding a new terminal building. On 10 September 1968, the new complex was opened and the west terminal became the cargo depot and the north terminal the general aviation centre. In 1976, fire gutted the north terminal. The old west terminal was then converted into a air commuter centre and strangely named the South Terminal.

Both Canadian Pacific and Trans-Canada, built maintenance complexes, cargo warehouses and hangars. Canadian Pacific named the road leading to its offices McConachie Way, after the man who had founded and nursed it for three decades.

As the airport expanded, the DOT expropriated more and more of Sea Island and predictably encountered the opposition of those who lived there. Soon, except for the

island. The local community was strongly opposed to further expansion and when a second runway was needed, fought to delay it for many years.

By the 1980s, Vancouver had positioned itself as the major entry point to North America for thousands of Asians. In competition with Seattle and San Francisco, the airport has waged a campaign to lure Japan Air Lines, Korean Air and Malaysian Airlines to fly into it. Another great crowd-puller were cruise ship passengers. As the closest airport for Alaskan cruise ships, Vancouver, to the chagrin of businessmen, seemed flooded with the thousands of cruise ship passengers transitting through the terminal to waiting buses.

When the federal government unveiled the National Airports Policy in 1992, Vancouver seized the opportunity to privatise. With the advent of the new Boeing 747s that could fly the Pacific non-stop, Vancouver recognised its potential as the Canadian gateway for the wealthy Asia-Pacific region. In what some might have said was unseemly haste, the Vancouver International Airport Authority took over management and plunged into an ambitious $400 million modernisation plan. After all, as a Pacific Rim airport Vancouver had to compete in efficiency and style with such giants as Singapore's Changi and Tokyo's Narita.

A $250 million terminal, a state of the art $14 million control tower and a new runway (opening in 1996) were all begun.

These improvements were none too soon, as by 1994 the terminal was handling 10.3 million passengers annually, or four times more than it was designed for. With the Open Skies Agreement, an extra 400,000 trans-border passengers were expected in 1995. The new terminal building is scheduled to open in June 1996 and will boost the airport's annual passenger-handling capacity to seventeen million travellers.

Proving that nothing comes without cost, the improvements are paid for by airline landing fees, duty-free shops and the infamous "Airport Improvement Fee." All passengers using Vancouver pay $10 for national flights and $15 for international trips. Although the airlines protest that they have to take the brunt of the passengers blame, the Airport Authority makes no apologies for the tax, claiming that it relieves congestion at the airport and that similar fees are inevitably going to be levied by other Canadian airports in the near future.

If the next century belongs to the countries on the Pacific Rim, Vancouver International can look to outdistancing Toronto and Montreal airports in all transportation.

Whitehorse

Whitehorse Airport was born as a landing site for four US Army aircraft in August, 1920. This was a long distance flight that the U.S. military mounted from New York to Nome, Alaska. The four De Havilland biplanes landed on a cleared lot of a hill above the frontier town of Whitehorse, returning there on their way back. The site of about 1,800 feet (549 metres) became the town's landing field for all the air traffic going to and from Alaska.

By the mid 1930s, aircraft had become the workhorses of the Arctic, ideal for traversing its inhospitable terrain. So many bushpilots began to use the Whitehorse airfield that the territorial government had the strip gravelled, lengthened and bisected it with a cross runway.

With the range and payload of aircraft ever increasing, Whitehorse airfield took on the role of a regular refuelling stop for air traffic between Fairbanks, Alaska and Seattle, W_____. The landing strip was widened to 1,600 feet

era. For a time, the White Horse Pass and Yukon Railway operated the airfield. In 1936, Pacific Alaska Airways (PAA), part of airline magnate Juan Trippe's empire, began flying their all metal Lockheed Electras into Whitehorse, connecting Fairbanks with the Alaskan state capital of Juneau. Because of the weight of the Lockheeds, the runways were asphalted and converted into all-weather use. PAA also installed a radio station and workshop at the airport.

Not to be outdone by the Americans, on 7 July, 1937, Grant McConachie, the president of United Air Transport Ltd. flew the first airmail between Edmonton and Whitehorse. The runway was extended to 4,500 feet (1,372 metres) and realigned into the prevailing wind. A second runway of 2,000 feet (610 metres) was built at right angles to the first.

Once America entered the Second World War, a secure transportation route through Canada to Alaska assumed a

ment for the duration of the war and extended the main
runway to 6,600 feet (2,012 metres) to better accommodate
the four-engined aircraft now using it. The RCAF and the
United States Air Force both built hangars on either side
of the airport and the USAF erected a large complex of
buildings on the west side of the airport. The United States
Navy took control of all Pacific Alaska Airways' operations.
By 1943, the air forces and airlines of both nations began
to replace their Lockheed Lodestars with DC-3s and, with
the war's end the four-engined DC-4s entered service.

When the USAF ended its ferrying through Whitehorse in 1945, the federal government bought their facilities for $8 million and moved the RCAF into them. All
civilian activities remained at the opposite side of the
airport with the old RCAF hangar. In 1961, a new terminal,
specifically designed for civilians, was constructed on the
west side. Tourism in the Yukon led to air charters, and the
search for mineral wealth meant that helicopter companies
began operations from the airport. In 1985, the old terminal
had become too congested and a new one was built. The
following year, 133,585 passengers passed through Whitehorse Airport and 53,228 aircraft used its runways. The
traffic was as varied as any border airport could be. Canadian Airlines' Boeing 737s, connecting the provincial capi

An eclectic collection of aircraft before the airport terminal in 1992. (Air
North Archives)

tal with Edmonton and Vancouver, shared apron space with
water bombers and RCMP aircraft.

At present, there are the three runways in use, the
longest being 23,760 by 495 feet (7,200 by 150 metres).
The airport provides employment for 111 people and in
1992 four scheduled airlines brought in 122,380 passengers. This was insufficient to make it financially economical
and that year it lost $1.5 million. Although it is currently
part of the National Airports System, federal financial
assistance will be phased out by 31 March, 2000 and Whitehorse Airport will be transferred to the territorial government under the Arctic Airports Transfer Plan.

Winnipeg

As early as 1919, there had been a few airfields around the City of Winnipeg. The British Canadian Aircraft Company operated from their own field in St. Charles, a suburb west of the city. In 1914, the three Macdonald brothers, Jim, Grant and Edwin, opened a sheet metal business on the banks of the Red River at the foot of Brandon Avenue. From it, Grant Macdonald used to watch bushpilots land their floatplanes. Soon he became friendly with aviators like Roy Brown, Punch Dickins and Wop May. Inevitably, he was asked to repair their floats, straighten propellers and rebuild their aircraft's wings. From these beginnings grew MacDonald Brothers Aircraft Ltd., that one day would become Bristol Aerospace Ltd.

In 1928, the Winnipeg Aeroplane Club leased 160 acres (64 hectares) of prairie from the municipality of St. James, a rural suburb of Winnipeg. On 27 May, Stevenson Aerodrome was formally opened on what would become

hero and bush pilot who had recently been killed in an air crash in Manitoba.

The Winnipeg Flying Club erected their own club house and hangars on the field. A year later, Western Canada Airways joined them at the airfield and built a large hangar and maintenance facility. With Winnipeg as its headquarters, the airline flew Fokker F-14s, Stearmans and Speedwing biplanes on airmail services to Calgary, Regina, Saskatoon and Edmonton. In February 1931, Northwest Airlines (later Northwest Orient) became the first international carrier to land at Stevenson Airport, connecting it with Pembina, North Dakota. Business for the American airline must have been good as it used a large Ford Trimotor, the jumbo jet equivalent of the era, on the route. As these were international flights, a Customs inspector became a permanent fixture at the airport.

In 1934, the RCAF established itself at the airfield,

Winnipeg Airport Bristol Aerospace Ltd., with its facilities to overhaul CF-5s. The company began in 1914 as a sheet metal business run by the MacDonald brothers on the banks of the Red River at Brandon Avenue. (Bristol Aerospace Archives)

Opened in 1964, the new terminal featured comfortable transit lounges and cafés that put Winnipeg on a par with American and European aiports. (Canadian Pacific Archives)

With the Depression, membership in the Winnipeg Flying Club gradually diminished and it went bankrupt. The club's run of bad luck continued as its only hangar twice burnt down, in 1937 and 1938. Finally, the club was forced to return the airport's lease to the Municipality of St. James for $2,500. But it remained to manage the site.

Winnipeg gained from the creation of the Trans-Canada Airway system in 1938. With it, federal funds were used

hangars and an office building. By 1939, there were boundary lights, a radio range station and a meteorological office. The Department of Transport also built three hard-surfaced runways: two 3,000 by 150 feet (915 by 46 metres), and one 3,200 by 150 feet (975 by 46 metres).

This was none too soon, as the year before Trans-Canada Airlines (TCA) made Winnipeg the centre of its training facilities. On the eve of the Second World War, TCA's Lockheed Electras began a scheduled passenger and mail service between Montreal, Toronto, Winnipeg and Vancouver.

With World War II, the Department of Transport took over the management of the airport from the Winnipeg Flying Club. The resident 112 Army Cooperation Squadron went overseas and converted to fighters. It flew Hurricanes in the Battle of Britain and later was renamed 402 Squadron RCAF.

As Trans-Canada Airlines had done, the British Commonwealth Air Training Plan (BCATP) made Winnipeg the main base for training on the prairies. Soon the airport was dotted with Elementary Flying Training Schools along with Wireless and Observer Schools. Thousands of Australian, New Zealand and British airmen were sent for training at Winnipeg. By 1940, the steady stream of bright yellow from the airport had become commonplace to local residents. The activity at the airport became a source of pride for the citizens of Winnipeg, and it has been said that no Canadian city had more affection for the thousands of BCATP personnel that passed through it.

The war also meant that aircraft manufacturing was stepped up at the airport. The BCATP Anson trainers were overhauled, and then built, by the MacDonald Brothers company, and Mid-West Aircraft made parts for Hurricanes. The Department of Munitions and Supply authorised the building of a factory for production of the Ansons on nearby Berry Street. The MacDonald plant had its own taxiway to the airport and, at its height, employed 4,500 people.

The Airport's reliance on the military continued in the postwar years. In 1948 two new runways were completed, 18-36 and 13-31. Both were 6,200 by 200 feet (1,890 by 61 metres) and equipped with the new Instrument Landing Systems. This came none too soon, as with the onset of the Korean and Cold Wars, there was once more a need for trained air crew and all basic training units were concentrated in Winnipeg. Number 2 Air Observer School became the largest in the country. Again, the airport facilities became home to personnel from many Allied (now NATO) countries. With the threat of Russian bombers flying over the North Pole, Winnipeg also became the supply point for the Distant Early Warning radar system in the far north.

Manufacturing at Winnipeg Airport suffered after the war when contracts for the Ansons ended, forcing MacDonald Aircraft to seek other markets. While continuing to overhaul war-surplus aircraft, the company displayed extreme resourcefulness by "making do" by reconditioning army trucks and building tractors and crop dusters. In 1949, an RCAF contract to rebuild Beechcraft Expeditors and North American Mustangs kept MacDonald Aircraft solvent, but just barely. On 30 July 1954 Bristol Aeroplane Co. of England bought the Winnipeg company for $3 million.

The civilian passenger facilities at the airport were also expanded and a new terminal building was opened on 15 December, 1952 to accommodate the offices of TCA and Northwest Orient. Sadly, in keeping with DOT policy, the airport's name was changed in 1959 from Stevenson Field to Winnipeg International Airport. As if to compensate for this, the pioneer aviator was commemorated with a statue inside the building.

With the arrival of TCA's DC-8 jet airliners in 1960, a new runway was built (07-25) and runway 13-31 extended. The 1952 terminal was by now proving too small for the crowds of passengers that the jet airliners brought in and in 1964, a new terminal complex was opened, surrounded by forty acres (16 hectares) of concrete apron. Passenger facilities, like the comfortable transit lounges and cafés, put Winnipeg airport on a par with airports in the United States and Europe. There were now twelve civilian hangers and, as the airport was a major air base for the RCAF, seven for the Air Force.

In 1966, the airport accommodated 630,000 passengers and no longer relied on the military for its employment. The expanding civil aviation sector was concentrated on the east side of the airport with the RCAF on the west. The Winnipeg Flying Club moved its operations to St. Andrew's Airport in 1977. That same year, two million passengers used the airport, making it the fifth busiest in Canada.

Bristol Aerospace was joined by Aero Recip Canada Ltd. and Douglas Aero Engine as manufacturing and overhaul companies at the airport. South of the expanded passenger terminal, cargo and maintenance depots were erected. Oil companies, the RCMP and the air freight companies also own facilities at the airport.

On Ferry Road, within view of the air traffic, is the Western Canada Aviation Museum. Possessing a Spitfire, a Vickers Vedette and a Junkers JU52-1M among its collection of historic aircraft, the museum boasts Canada's largest aviation bookstore.

In 1992, sixteen scheduled airlines used Winnipeg International Airport, transporting 2,142,124 passengers. On the basis of this traffic and because it serves the provincial capital, Winnipeg is part of the National Airports System. Over 4,500 people work at the airport and of the three runways in use the longest is 36,300 by 660 feet (11,000 by 200 metres) in length.

The airport operates at a considerable financial surplus. With flight training, aircraft maintenance and corporate and charter operations expanding, it is expected to continue to do so. The largest scheduled aircraft using Winnipeg Airport today is Air Canada's Boeing 747, a far cry from the Lockheed Electras and Stearmans of its early days.

Yellowknife

The initial attraction of Yellowknife was as a base for mineral exploration in remote northern areas. The two gold mines discovered nearby are still operating, and the spinoffs such as exploration, service and retail continue to make the airport a busy one.

The origins of Yellowknife Airport are associated with two of Canada's aviation pioneers. In 1933, Walter Gilbert had won the Trans-Canada Trophy for his exploratory flights in the North. A decade later, he was the district manager of Canadian Pacific Air Lines during the CANOL (Canadian Oil) Project and told to build an airport at Yellowknife. Gilbert had a site surveyed four kilometres (2.40 miles) from the town, then hired six men to clear a strip of land, parallel to Long Lake, for the airfield.

When the airport opened, there was still no road to the town and passengers were put aboard a floatplane which shuttled back and forth. This was remembered as the "elo vator trip" because the aircraft went up and then down so dramatically. In 1945, the Department of Transport

awarded Matt Berry the contract to build a road from the settlement to the airport. The media had bestowed on Berry the title "King of the Northern Fliers" and he was already famous for the several hazardous flights made to the Arctic Coast in the 1930s. The legendary bush pilot found out that the United States Army Engineers, having just completed the CANOL pipeline, were at a loss as to what to do with their bulldozers, trucks and graders. It is not known which of the two parties was more grateful, but Berry took the heavy equipment and completed the road, expanding the Canadian Pacific airfield as well.

A year later, the Department of Transport took over the airport from Canadian Pacific and chose another site half a kilometre from the original. Berry had by now formed his own airport construction company and was given the job. On 13 May, 1946, his bulldozers began levelling the area and two gravel strips, one north–south and one northwest–southeast were laid out. On 28 August 1947, no less a personage than W.M. Neal, President and Chairman of the

Canadian Pacific Railway, flew into Yellowknife to officiate at the opening of the airport. With him was Grant McConachie, President of Canadian Pacific Air Lines. Soon, the DC-3s of Northern Flights Ltd and Canadian Pacific Air Lines began to service Yellowknife.

No history of Yellowknife Airport would be complete without recognising the achievements of Max Ward. In 1946, the young Ward was flying for Northern Flights Ltd., but quit to begin his own charter service at Yellowknife Airport. His Polaris Charter Company of Yellowknife consisted of a single Fox Moth, but with it he carried prospectors and supplies to camps in the area. In 1952, despite setbacks, Ward took delivery of a De Havilland Otter and began Wardair Ltd. The Territories were in the middle of a prospecting frenzy and Wardair flew drill crews, fuel and food from Yellowknife to the very fringes of the Arctic. In 1957, a Bristol Freighter was added to the fleet to carry heavy equipment — from tractors to cows, medicine to floor lamps, even the neighbourhood fire engine — throughout the Northwest Territories. It was only in 1961 that Ward moved his airline's headquarters out of Yellowknife to Edmonton and began concentrating on holiday charters.

As the workhorse of the north, the DC-3 remains a familiar sight at Yellowknife airport. DC-3s of Canadian Pacific Airlines began using the airport's unpaved runway in 1947. (Air North Archives)

for their polar photographic surveys. It became necessary to pave the runways for heavier aircraft to land on them. In April 1954, 120 tons (121.92 metric tons) of construction equipment was brought in from Hay River by tractor-train across the ice of Great Slave Lake. The trip took three and half days, a record necessitated by the spring thaw.

Yellowknife Airport temporarily became part of the

Yellowknife airport temporarily became part of the Soviet Union in 1955. The airport was closed and used as a target by airborne Canadian Army units and the RCMP.

Yellowknife achieved some fame as it was designated by Canadian Pacific Airlines as alternate airport on their non-stop Vancouver-Amsterdam flights. In 1963 a terminal was built and a new control tower added in 1972. Both facilities were completely renovated in 1989.

Today the largest scheduled aircraft to use the airport is a Boeing 727. Besides Canadian North, Yellowknife is served by Buffalo Airways, Ptarmigan Airways, Northwest Territorial Air, First Air and Air Tindi. The airport celebrated its fiftieth anniversary in 1994, and the Fox Moths and Bellancas have been replaced with Hercules and Twin Otters, the scheduled DC-3s with Boeing 737s. The airport has increased from one local operator and one southern connector to ten local operators and three southern connectors. Because of the uniqueness of the community, the scheduled carriers have had to adapt their aircraft and services. For example, the Boeing 737s that use Yellowknife have large overhead cargo doors enabling them to place 6,000 pound (2,700 kilogram) containers of freight in the cabin after the seats have been removed. The airport incurred its most serious deficit of $2.1 million in 1992. As part of the National Airports System, federal financial assistance will be phased out by 31 March 2000. As over 200,000 people use Yellowknife Airport annually, with an average of fifty scheduled flights per week, it might be an attractive option when, as an Arctic Airport, it will be made available for transfer to the territorial government.

Conclusion

It is a warm summer's evening in 1995 and a family is driving to the airport. They could be in Montreal, Toronto, Vancouver or Winnipeg. As their minivan edges through the traffic on the airport freeway, they notice the incoming planes, appearing in the hazy sky.

There is no pleasure in this trip. They are going to meet someone, not gawk at aircraft. The father is already worrying about which parking space to use: is the short term for stays under two hours better than the long term, which is cheaper but a five minute bus ride from the terminal? The most anyone in the car will actually see of an aircraft is a distant DC-9 taxiing about three kilometres away. Through the traffic haze looms one of the terminal buildings. It is an attractive structure of several concourses that manages to convey its architect's intention of a mother ship for circling sharks. No longer capped by a control tower, which now sits

I (or II or III) might be the corporate headquarters of an up-market computer company.

For the general public, airports have become necessary evils and their architecture passes quickly out of mind; planes land, planes take off, people get on and people get off. At some point in the last thirty years, we became numbed to their appeal. Formerly the gateways to an utopian future, airports are now synonymous with stress, bedlam and random suspicion. It is ironic that fear of flying was replaced by fear of one's fellow passengers. Like the meanest city street or border post, airports have become the nation's first line of combat, a daily no-man's-land in the war against terrorists, drug smugglers and illegal immigrants.

Then too, the airport authorities have long since made it very clear that their workplaces are too dangerous for family picnics and sightseers. Few airports even have the

times, the dimensions of airport concourses have been calculated by accountants, not visionaries. At peak hours (from 7:00 to 9:30 A.M., and from 3 to 10 P.M.), they are not places for anyone other than passengers and employees. No longer picnic sites or theme parks to aerial transportation, airports have become places of business like any office building or industrial park.

For the family, their first impressions through the sliding doors of the terminal building are of endlessly milling crowds and chaos. Standing in the concourse beside the tacky souvenir stands festooned with "My Parents Went To . . . and All I Got Was . . ." t-shirts, the family sees more ethnic groups stream past them than they thought lived in Canada.

After the first wide-bodied airliner was put into service, the airport became a transit point for the whole country and the world: here the wealthy and the starving collide, the serious and the shady mingle for a few minutes before returning to their corners. Because of who they attract, each airport has its own beat. The rhythm of one in the Arctic is noticeably different from that of Dorval or Pearson. For more than in its streets and neighbourhoods, this is where all the elements of the community's mythology come together.

In the last years of this century, the drama is no longer about the technology outside the terminal but the humanity within. Microwave precision landing systems, airfield surface movement radar and Combi B747s pale in comparison to the theatre within.

The family squeezes around the lines that snake up to ticket counters. They step around the overstuffed luggage carts shepherded by excited vacationers. Periodically, the "Arrivals" doors will burst open to pour out puffy-eyed people eager to be home, pushing dirty laundry and sleeping children before them. Having made sense of the venetian-blind Flight Arrival Board, the parents pull their children out of the coin arcade and head towards one of the six food outlets in the terminal. Invariably called "The Food Court," it ranges from a self-service cafeteria to a 1970s style hotel lounge with waitress service. The family settles for the junk food concession with its themed early aviation motif. Here, blownup photos of J.A.D. McCurdy taking off at Baddeck Bay compete for attention with the latest Disney creations.

Across from them, the moving sidewalk deposits dishevelled passengers who are uniformly red-eyed and dazed, easy marks for local pickpockets, fraud artists and taxi drivers. People struggle to control luggage carts piled high with suitcases, cardboard boxes and shopping bags. But the family barely sees them, unimpressed with the fact that, a

Once gateways to an utopian future, large airports are now synonymous with stress, bedlam and random suspicion. (Aeroports de Montréal photo)

few hours before, these walking dead were in Miami, Glasgow, Rio and Hawaii.

Out of their sight, the real airport dramas are taking place. No longer for the very rich or the very brave, flying has become democratized. Among the tourists and businessmen at the airport are drug smugglers and refugees, the desperate and the naive. Behind the concourse's opaque ... have become suspicious of

too much luggage for a vacation. When questioned, the illegal immigrants break down and blame the "tour operator" who took their money and has already faded away into the crowds.

Illegal entry is a growing problem at all Canadian airports and, as guardians of the national mood, the immigration officers have seen it all. Fake passports, photo alteration, valid pages stitched into fake passports, fake pages in valid passports, counterfeit visas and more. The airport has truly become the gateway of the poor and dispossessed to the Promised Land.

There are no longer public announcements of aircraft arrivals or departures. Studies have shown that most people do not listen to them anyway. And if there were, who would care? The news that Lufthansa is leaving for Frankfurt or Cathay Pacific has arrived from Hong Kong, triumphs of technology, the stuff of dreams thirty years ago, would be met with boredom.

High above the crowds in the control tower, controllers guide a constant stream of air traffic. Leaving aside the DC-10s and Airbuses, Pearson alone handles twenty-two 747s daily. Born not long after the miracles of radio-teleph- ... systems that

Trillium Terminal Three, Lester B. Pearson International Airport (DHA Architects International Inc. photo)

are aircraft as varied in speed and mission as the Concorde or Hercules.

There is one persistent announcement over the public address system. It concerns leaving baggage unattended. Airports have become prime targets not only for luggage snatchers and con artists but terrorists as well. The first aircraft in history to be blown up by a bomb in its hold was a Quebec Airways DC-3 in 1949. Canadian airports have not been immune to the spate of hijackings and mass mid-air murder that put Lod and Mogadishu airports on our television screens. Long before Lockerbie, metal detectors and sniffer dogs became part of every airport's equipment. The 1985 Air India tragedy originated too close to home and caused a national paranoia as our vulnerability to terrorism replaced the old fear of flying.

On Runway 27 Right, a 775,000 pound (348,750 kilogram) mass of metal made by McDonnell-Douglas lifts off. It is a moment dramatic enough to have been part of science fiction a half century ago. But except for a lone airtug tractor driver, no one has watched the Martinair DC-10 climb into the haze. There is a bittersweet poignancy to this. Despite the fact that the world's civil aviation fleet has gone from 3,000 aircraft in 1946 to over 18,000 in 1991, air transportation, in statistical terms, has never been safer, more efficient or more comfortable. Yet potted palms and inter-faith chapels aside, most airports have never been less user-friendly or cheerless than they are today. This is not the forum to discuss why this happened.

The world's indifference to the marvel of flight can only be compared with its attitude to the later Apollo flights. Once the lofty aspirations to fly had been achieved and the oceans conquered, we moved on.

Did our parents or grandparents really spend their Sunday afternoons thrilled by the ear-splitting roar of a Ford Trimotors' engines and being showered with dust and grime at the edge of a grubby field? Airports have done more than provide a location for aerial transport. They have affected our national economics, changed our social and cultural points of view and, if the two world wars are any yardstick, they have had a hand in shaping the course of our political history. Throughout this history, there is a constant: there is no such thing as an immutable

Despite pollution, terrorism and congestion, airports remain what they were designed to be: everyone's launch pad, our gateways to the world. (Roth and Ramberg Photography)

Bibliography

Although the National Archives were extensively used, this book could not have been written without continous reference to Tom McGrath's *The History of Canada's Airports* Toronto: Lugus Publications, 1983. Mr. McGrath witnessed aviation evolving in this country. As a child in Newfoundland he actually saw the aircraft of both Alcock and Brown and Admiral Kerr. Later, he was posted to Gander Airport in its earliest days.

Other sources used were:

The National Archives: Airports RG 12, Finding Aid 12-23, Part 2.

Ellis, Frank H. *Canada's Flying Heritage* Toronto: University of Toronto Press, 1954.

Greif, Martin *The Airport Book* Toronto : Beaverbooks, 1979.

Long, C.D. "Toronto Airports Before Malton" *CAHS Journal*, Winter 1965

Main, J.R.K. *Voyageurs of the Air: A History of Civil Aviation in Canada 1858 1967* Ottawa: Queen's Printer, 1967.

Milberry, Larry *Aviation in Canada* Toronto: McGraw-Hill Ryerson 1979

Sullivan, K. & Milberry L. Power. *The Pratt & Whitney Story* Toronto. CANAV Books 1989

Wilson, J.A. *Development of Aviation in Canada 1879 1910* Ottawa: King's Printer, 1948.